Tempus ORAL HISTORY *Series*

Rutland
voices

Workmen preparing the land around Hambleton for flooding and in due course creating Rutland Water.

Tempus ORAL HISTORY *Series*

Rutland
voices

Compiled by
Judith Spelman

TEMPUS

Tempus Publishing Limited
The Mill, Brimscombe Port,
Stroud, Gloucestershire, GL5 2QG

ISBN 0 7524 2156 5

Typesetting and origination by
Tempus Publishing Limited
Printed in Great Britain by
Midway Clark Printing, Wiltshire

Acknowledgements

I am grateful to all the people who spent so much time talking to me about their earliest memories. This, along with the many personal photographs loaned to me, provides all the material for this book. I also thank the *Stamford Mercury* for permission to use some photographs.

Contents

Foreword   6

Introduction   7

1.   Early Days   9

2.   Schooldays   21

3.   House and Home   35

4.   Games We Played   45

5.   Off to Work   52

6.   High Days and Holidays   62

7.   Village Life   74

8.   Town Talk   105

9.   People and Places   120

Foreword

There have been three occasions when Rutland almost lost its county status. I think it was first mooted just before the First World War, then in the 1960s Leicestershire County Council made a bid to take over Rutland which failed. The police forces merged to become the Leicestershire and Rutland Police Force, which it still is today, but the county held onto its county status in other things, including education, which was always felt to be far superior to that of Leicestershire's! In those early days some people would undertake two positions because the duties that they entailed were relatively small. For example if an area has its own police force, the Chief Constable was also Education Attendance Officer. There was a situation where everybody had a dual job in the old county council. The economy of scale was always in everyone's minds; Rutland was a very frugal county council that did not spend any more money than it needed to.

In 1974 there was a big reorganization of local government. An enquiry was held in the Castle at Oakham, which at that time was the Assize Court, and this lasted two or three weeks. At the end of the day it was ruled that Rutland should merge with Leicestershire, and this was considered to be pretty sad by many people. A large majority did not want it, although some felt that it might create better services – at the time there was not much money available for things like buses. Rutland County Council was largely made up of farmers, but there was also a railway worker from Ketton and another who used to cycle to council meetings. The meetings took place at half past nine on Wednesdays mornings and at noon the meeting would break up and they would all go across to the Crown Hotel where refreshments were laid on. Lord Gainsborough used to regale us with stories.

I was chairman of the council for four years – two successive terms. I was there when we won our county status back. The government decided to form new unitary councils, but there was a lot of scepticism and people said it would be for the big cities but the Prime Minister, John Major, said that they were planning to form some unitary councils from very small authorities. We thought this was good because although we could get our county back, we were concerned that we would be able to obtain sufficient funds to do so. We sought assurances on that basis and then we formed a group made up of Andrew Makey, a farmer from Edith Weston, Eddie Martin, who was a master at Oakham School, Pat Holloway and myself to address the situation.

We met the commissioners on a number of occasions when they came to review Leicestershire. We had suggested initially that it would be a good idea if Rutland and Stamford were to form a unitary council, perhaps going as far as the Deepings or even Bourne. It made sense because much of the economic and social movement, certainly on the east side, went towards Stamford rather than Oakham. We thought it would be sensible to look at that option. But the commissioners had a brief with many strictures and they were not allowed to cross existing county boundaries even though they considered it viable. Then out of the blue came a recommendation that we should reconsider our unitary status. There was a lot of opposition from notable people in Leicestershire especially as Leicester City was applying for unitary status. We went to London to hear the debate in Parliament. Lord Gainsborough, one of our members spoke, and the Leader of the Opposition, Baroness Hollis, was obviously in favour as well as a number of the Conservatives. They debated for about two hours and eventually voted in favour.

Brian Montgomery
Former Chairman of Rutland County Council 1992-1993, 1997-1998.

Introduction

When I was a child living in the West Country, I was taught that Rutland was the smallest county in England. That made it special, and over the years I have realised how special it is for people who live here. Even when the government of the day removed its county status, Rutlanders continued to end their addresses with 'Rutland, Leicestershire'. They are very proud of their heritage, and indeed, it is a unique county.

This book is made up of memories and treasured photographs from people who have spent most of their lives in Rutland. Many were born and bred here, moving from one town or village to another, and others have spent a significant part of their lives in the county. A few have retired elsewhere but their memories for the places in the county where they spent so many years, and for the people they knew many years ago, are still strong.

These are memories that go back well into the early part of the twentieth century, spanning sixty, seventy, eighty and sometimes ninety years. They show how daily life has changed, how things that we take for granted nowadays were often unavailable years ago and how values have altered. There were distinct roles for men and women and once married, the man was considered to be the provider and the woman looked after the house and the children. What emerges so clearly from my long conversations with Rutland people is the difference between town and village. Transport was minimal and it was considered normal to walk several miles to shop in the town and walk back with your purchases. Children thought nothing of walking two or three miles to school and when they grew up, they cycled or walked even greater distances to work and back. Life was physically harder in the villages but there was still time to have fun!

The week had a pattern for the housewife: Monday was washday, Tuesday was ironing, Wednesday meant cleaning, and so on. Anne Spencer told me proudly that it would take her all morning to make a good stew and May Wright remembered cleaning the knives with Bathbrick on a Saturday. Everything took so long to do. Washing was easier if you had a copper that you could light a fire under and boil the dirty linen, but if you had just an open fire and a tin bowl that would only take a sheet at a time, that was a different matter. Some eighty years ago, few people had running water in the kitchen or even the luxury of a sink. Housework in those days was, quite simply, hard work.

Listening to someone telling tales of years ago has always fascinated me. I remember my grandmother and great aunts talking about their lives as young girls in a large household. Life was so different yet if we attempted to do all the things they did during a typical day, we would never do the things we take for granted and consider essential now. Talking to people like this brings home the truth that unless you know about the past you cannot fully understand the present.

We know about major events that affected everyone nationally or locally – wars, the cold winters, National Service, the regular town shows, the changes in transport – because these are well documented by historians and archivists. What we do not know is how people dealt with these situations, how they lived through them and how they were affected. This is the value of an oral history book such as this and the bonus is that once older people begin to look at it, their own memories come flooding back. I know of families that have been reunited because of a chance purchase of one of these Voices books that included a photo of a great-grandparent.

Talking about the past is almost as popular as talking about the weather but it is important to realise that memory can be extraordinarily fickle and selective. Over a number of years, people, places and events can become a little blurred There may well be some incidents described that differ quite a bit from others. I cannot guarantee the accuracy of the

As the horses trek home from ploughing along a lane in Belmersthrope, baker Bill Smith and his assistant, Aubrey Turner are deliverig bread to local houses. The bakery, Proctor Bros, ws based in Stamford and Bill delivered round many Rutland villages. This photograph is thought to have been taken one winter in the early 1940s and ws lent by Roger Smith, Bill's son.

recollections in this book although I have tried to check spellings and dates carefully.

The people who kindly spent time talking to me for this book come from all parts of the county and were chosen at random. I began by talking to Maurice Wade who was born in Barrowden. He said I must speak to Robin Ellis who mentioned what I was doing to someone else and so it went on. A friend living in Bedfordshire told me her father and grandparents lived for many years in Oakham so I went to see him in Shrewsbury and you will discover that Eddie Butcher's memories are as vivid as ever. When I met Eileen Snow she spoke about Eddie as a childhood friend and was amazed I had met him. May Wright spent her childhood in Empingham and knew Arthur Branson well so I had to tell her all about him. 'He was a real artist, you know,' she told me. It is meeting people in this way and managing to find links that make compiling a book like this so rewarding. There are many others I would love to have involved in this book but somehow our paths did not cross.

I am indebted to the many people who helped and encouraged me to write this book. There are many excellent books on Rutland including histories of the county and books of personal memories. I hope this book will be a useful addition and bring back even more memories of Rutland to the reader.

Judith Spelman
September 2000

CHAPTER 1
Early Days

Annie Gatehouse and Albert Butcher were in service together before they were married. Annie is second from the left in the middle row and Albert is on the right in the back row. They married at The Little Church Around the Corner in New York and eventually came to run the Cross Keys in Oakham.

Rinsed in Vinegar

I was Monica Wiggington and I was born in Whissendine. My father was the blacksmith and I had three brothers, Bill, Arthur and Fred. I lost my mother when I was four years old. She died in the 1918 flu epidemic. We had people coming in to look after the house and look after us but they didn't live in. I remember there was Mary Ellis – 'Omis' we used to call her. Omis used to cook for us. On our way home from school at twelve o'clock

Mr Birch and Pixie outside the house in Wing where his son, Raymond, was born.

we used to call at her house and collect our meal. Omis used to wash my hair. We didn't have shampoo so I think she just used soap and then she would rinse it with vinegar. If there was any lice in the school she used to put some Lysol in the water. When I had long hair she used to put it in rags. These were long pieces of rag which were twice the length of your hair. One rag was wound round your hair and the other piece was wound round again over the top and then tied at the bottom. I hated it because it wasn't very comfortable and I had to sleep in these rags. So my brother cut my hair.

Monica Leclere

Long Curly Hair

I can remember screaming as a child because I hated having my hair washed. Once a neighbour from across the way came running over to see what was the matter. I had long curly hair as a child but if you had straight hair there were irons you put in the fire and when they were hot you would wind them round your hair to make it curl.

I was born at Preston and I went to school there and then to Uppingham Central School. My dad was a farmer and our house was Wing's Farm. There were six of us in the family and my father had come to the farm in about 1913.

Gladys Birch

The Steps

I was born in Burley next door to where I live now. It was called The Steps in those days. It was a private estate and one of the very first things I can remember was the estate children's Christmas party. It was held at the mansion that belonged to Mr Finch. He used to hold an annual part for the children which was in a great big room with big stairs. Underneath the stairs was a doll's house and that made such an impression on me. I would be about four years old at the time. I had never seen a doll's house as big as that before. I can't remember much about the party but I know there was a Christmas tree and presents. They were ever so good to the workers. The party was organized by Miss Jasmine, Mr Finch's sister, and she handed out the presents. When Mr Finch died in 1939, the parties stopped.

Ray Hill

Touching Your Cap

If the parson or Major Hesketh came to see us, you always had to touch your cap.

George Goodwin

'Pet' Pawlett

Most people don't know me by my real name! I was born Eileen Pawlett but I was always known as 'Pet' Pawlett. My brother gave me that when I was four. My grandfather, Henry Pawlett, used to look after Cutts Close in Oakham when I was a child. We lived at No. 7 John Street and they lived at No. 10. John Street is still there but where we lived was pulled down and the Somerfield supermarket was built. The Cross Keys was there and that was

Ray Hill with his father.

pulled down. When the Butchers left the Cross Keys my uncle, Tom King, took over the pub. My brother George and I were friendly with Eddie Butcher and his sister Violet. Eddie was friendly with Mrs Richardson who lived at No. 17. I remember the Butchers had a rocking horse.

I was born in a house in John Street. You went up two steps to get to the front door and that led straight into the living room. There was another room and then what we called the back kitchen which had the stove and the boiler. The toilet was in the yard and just outside the back door was a tap. There was a covered-in passage at the side of the house which joined onto the next house. In the passage there was an old wooden pump that was used before we had

tap water and this served several houses. There was no running water in our house and we had to use the tap outside and collect it in buckets and bowls and jugs. We heated it on a small range and we had a gas stove.

Eileen Snow

Regular Bedtime

I was born in Lower Hambleton which is under the water now, but we soon moved to Oakham in Parkfield Road where there were all new houses. I had six brothers and one sister and I remember we always had to be in at a regular time for bed. I was the third youngest. My eldest sister used to come out of the house and shout each of our names loudly – John, Joyce, Eunice! Bedtime!

Eunice Hill

Evacuees

I was an orphan and when I was a ten-year old lad I was fostered out in South Luffenham and I lived the rest of my life in Rutland. I was found abandoned at The Ashes in Oakham which was the workhouse and I was fostered by Charles Henry Hudson and his wife, Rosetta who lived in a little terraced house at No. 3 Flower Terrace. I was with them until I got married. They used to take in evacuee boys because they didn't have any family of their own and so they thought it would be nice to foster a child. I went to live with them about 1944. In those early days there was no running water and I used to have to go to the middle of the village with a yoke over my shoulders and two buckets which I would fill from the spring. I brought them home and filled the various vessels. Outside we had a water butt for the rainwater and a tank to put in the spring water for drinking. Then there were buckets inside the house to fill.

Everyone used to keep a pig at the end of the garden and when it was killed it was put on a scratch in the pantry. A scratch was a wooden board which sloped into the centre with handles on the side. The butcher, 'Bitty' Lake, would come from Wing and he would butcher the pig and cut it into hams and flitches. We had a long pantry where we used to keep the meat. We used to rub salt all over the hams, and the flitches used to be

Percival Strafford with his daughter Dorothy outside a barn in Aldgate, Ketton, c. 1905.

laid in flat trays and salted. That would keep them. When the pig was being fattened up, all the people in the village who didn't have pigs would bring their scraps to help feed it and then they'd know they'd get a bit of the pig later! My job was to take around what was called the Pig's Fry. That was a mixture of kidney, liver, belly pork with bacon on the top and I would take a plateful covered with a napkin. Some people would give me sixpence, others might give me a piece of bread and jam.

Mrs Hudson used to make pork pies. She used to make sausages as well, in fact she used to make everything! There was only one thing I didn't like and that was the chitterlings. They were made from the intestines and I remembered what it was like

Mrs Rosetta Hudson in South Luffenham.

cleaning them out! What I did like was the collared head or the brawn. Nobody could make brawn like Mrs Hudson!

Alan Fox

Salting the Pig

The dairy was big and it faced north so it was always cool there. When we killed the pig, that was where the salting was done. It was always my job when we killed the pig to crush a huge bar of salt. I remember I used a blunt knife to cut the salt into pieces and then I crushed it with a rolling pin. I always helped cut the leaf for rendering into lard. The leaf is the fat that lies inside the pig. You take it out and cut it into little pieces and put it in a deep dish. When the oven was fairly cool, you put the dish in and the

Nellie Clark, daughter of Dick Clark, on her pony at the back of the Falcon in Uppingham.

fat melted into pure lard. We put it into jars and covered them with greaseproof paper ready for when my mother wanted some for baking.

Elsie Rose

The Last One Left

I was born at Martinsthorpe at the old farm. Martinsthorpe House, we called it. There have been Bransons at Martinsthorpe since 1850. I was born in 1908 and I'm the only Branson left who was born there.

Arthur Branson

Rabbit Food

We used to keep rabbits which were a cross between Flemish Giant and Belgian Hare so a rabbit weighed between eight and nine pounds. We used to supply the American Air Force with twenty-five to thirty rabbits a week. One of my jobs was to go out every night with two sacks to fill with rabbit food – dandelions and cow parsley and sour thistle.

Alan Fox

Preserving Potatoes

I used to help Charlie Hudson on his allotment and I was not allowed to go and play until we'd finished. He'd preserve the potatoes for winter by 'clamping' them. He'd dig a hole and lay straw out on the bottom. Then he would bring a column of straw up the centre and pile the potatoes round it into a pyramid shape. He'd pack straw all the way round and that way the potatoes could breathe. Charlie Hudson used to grow marigolds, the old-fashioned sort, in amongst the cabbages and that used to stop the butterflies laying eggs.

We had a big larder, which we called the dairy. Every morning before I went to school I had to go down to John Bellamy's farm and collect the milk in billycans for us and the neighbours. I used to get 3d a week for doing that.

Alan Fox

Collecting Milk

We used to go and collect our milk in a can every day from Bolton's farm which was on the main street in Barrowden. Milk was delivered to some people from Church Farm. They used a horse and pony trap. They put the churns on and filled your cans from them. It crushed my three-wheeler trike one day!

The butchers were called Woods and they were near to the bakehouse on the second green from where I lived, although there was a slaughterhouse in between the two.

Maurice Wade

Good Raw Milk

I was born in the old maltings at No. 46 High Street, Uppingham. My father was born there, in the same room. My grandfather

John Tabrum aged about three on a pony.

came to Uppingham in the late 1880s to manage a farm for Mrs Watt. When she died he bought her farm. Back in the 1850s I think John Wadd was the maltster. When I was young the old malt ovens were still there. I have the scales they used to use for weighing the malt stacks.

My father was a dairy farmer and we had Shorthorns when I was little and then we had Friesians in the 1950s. We packed up the dairy in the early 1960s. We had a farm yard on both sides of the road and we used to walk the cows up and down the road to the fields, twice a day in the winter and four times a day in the summer. They were milked and the milk was bottled and delivered around the town. My father used to start milking at six and then he would go off with the first round of milk at about half past seven. That would be last night's milk, which would have been cooled. The morning's milk was taken after breakfast as a second delivery. He went to a different part of the town. The school houses wanted their milk fairly early. If we had any surplus then a lorry used to come at about eleven o'clock in the morning and pick it up. We used to leave it in churns on a stand at the side of the road. It was good raw milk, never pasteurised.

John Tabrum

No Sewing or Knitting

On Sundays there was always church. Church in the morning, Sunday School in the afternoon and church again at night. We weren't allowed to sew or knit on Sundays but we could read. Our Sunday lunch was usually roast beef and Yorkshire pudding followed by a milk pudding. When I was about four or five I had an uncle, Len Scotchbrook, who was blind. His father kept the coal yard near the station. Every Sunday morning I took him to church.

Georgina Andrews

A Muddy Lane

I was born at Ridlington, which is about ten miles away from where I live now in North Luffenham. I was born at Rowells Lodge which belonged to my grandfather. It was an old farmhouse with no road to it, just a muddy land and I lived there until I was about fifteen. My mother kept house for my grandfather. It was quite a large house. There were five bedrooms, a sitting room, a big old kitchen, a dairy at the back and a cellar underneath the dairy. There was also a very big garden. My grandfather was a farm worker but he kept two or three cows, some chickens and a pig.

I used to go to the farm where my grandfather worked most days and fetch the milk. It was about a pint and I collected it in a tin can with a handle at the top. No bottles on the doorstep in those days!

Elsie Rose

Elsie Rose as a child in Ridlington.

Grace and George Goodwin, aged six and eight respectively, in 1918.

Coachman

When I first came to Rutland in 1919, I lived at Stocken Hall. I was eight when we came, my sister and I, with my mother and my grandparents. My father was killed in 1914. My grandfather got a job as coachman and stud groom at Stocken Hall for Major Fleetwood Hesketh. He got the job because he had two grandchildren who could go to Stretton school and so helped keep it from being closed.

George Goodwin

Helping the Farmer

I remember helping the farmer next door get the crew yard, where the cattle were kept during the winter, sorted out. We had to get all the manure out and load it on a trailer to go up to the fields. That was in the spring.

Maurice Wade

Fireworks

When I was about ten or twelve, I used to get up in the morning and go down the stables

From left to right, back row: M. Charles Wortley, owner of Ridlington House, and Christopher Rowell. Front row: Mr Gray and Mr Rudkin of Uppingham. The photograph was taken in the 1920s after the men had received their long service awards.

to muck out and groom two ponies. Then at the weekend I was allowed to ride one of the hunters on exercise. In those days you had to carry water. I would go down to the village pump with a bucket. As children we used to play with the Hesketh children on the lawn at Stocken Hall. I was taught how to ride a bike and how to shoot.

There used to be parties for people who worked on the estate and Major Hesketh would put on firework displays.

George Goodwin

Egleton and then along some other fields to Lower Hambleton and then into Middle Hambleton. When the buses started running, we'd go to Hambleton because my auntie lived at the post office. The way we walked it was about four miles and it took us about an hour and a half. We went to the Stamford road to catch the bus back and there was a seat there which used to say 'wait till the bus rolls by'. We used to sit on that until the United Counties bus came

Eileen Snow

Waiting Till the Bus Rolled By

When we were children we'd walk from Oakham to Hambleton where we had family. We went up the Albion road to Mount Pleasant, cut through the fields to

Doris Pawlett with her children, George and 'Pet' (Eileen), on one of the regular walks they did from Oakham to Hambleton.

CHAPTER 2
Schooldays

A stone was laid in the school wall at Ketton which states that in 1932, sixty-two square yards of schoolyard were given to widen the road.

Tricks

I went to South Luffenham village school when the head teacher was Miss Tebbutt. Mrs Bussingham was the cook and whenever it was anybody's birthday, she would cook their favourite pudding. I used to like chocolate which was hard to get but she used to manage it. There used to be a long slanting roof and like a coping stone all along the edges. One of my favourite tricks was to run up over the roof and click the bell and get down before the teacher came out. I could run up there, click the bell and be down the other side before the teacher even thought of coming out!

Alan Fox

Eddie Butcher at Oakham School.

Starting With a Hymn

When I went to the village school in Whissendine, it was down by the green but now it has been made into a private house. There were only two rooms in the school and there were four teachers. Mr Newsham was the headmaster and there was Mrs Stafford, Mrs Dexter and Miss Robespierre. We got to school at nine and we always started the day with a hymn and prayers. We sat on long forms at desks that were sometimes in twos or fours. When we started to write, we first learnt to print. Then we learnt to join up the print into writing. When we first started we used slates to write on and a slate pencil. When we were ready to write with a pen on paper, we had a wooden pen that you dipped into ink. You got blots on your fingers and the ink was all over the place! We learnt to knit in the infants and as you went up you learnt to sew. I think I made an apron. I can remember us all having to go out in the yard at the back of the school with our toothbrushes and mugs and we had to clean our teeth.

I passed the scholarship but I finished up at the private school in the village known as Miss Stafford's School. It was just before you get to the church. It was a private house but she had a school room at the back.

Monica Leclere

Pens with Square Nibs

We sat at desks with lids and inkwells. When I went to Oakham Central School which was on Cold Overton Road we did italic writing and had lessons using pens with square nibs. I enjoyed it and I was quite good at it.

Christine Baum

A Glass Eye

When I went to Oakham Central School we used to go across the fields to the station at Luffenham. I used to leave home at quarter past eight and stop for a friend who was never up! We had to run across the station fields to get the train and if the driver saw us, he'd wait for us. If we missed the train coming home, we would walk from Oakham along the railway line. That was the quickest way.

The headmaster was Bobbie Cartwright. He had a glass eye and when he looked at you, you didn't know which it was. He was a very fair, and a very good headmaster.

Alan Fox

For the High Jump

I went first to the old junior school which was opposite Oakham church and opposite the Wheatsheaf pub. There's now a car park where the school stood. Old Dorsey Ellingworth taught at the junior school in Oakham. She was a real character in Oakham. She was small and wore glasses and she played the piano. Everybody was frightened of the headmaster, Mr Bracegirdle. They say that before he came to Oakham he was headmaster of a reform school! I was very good at high jump and

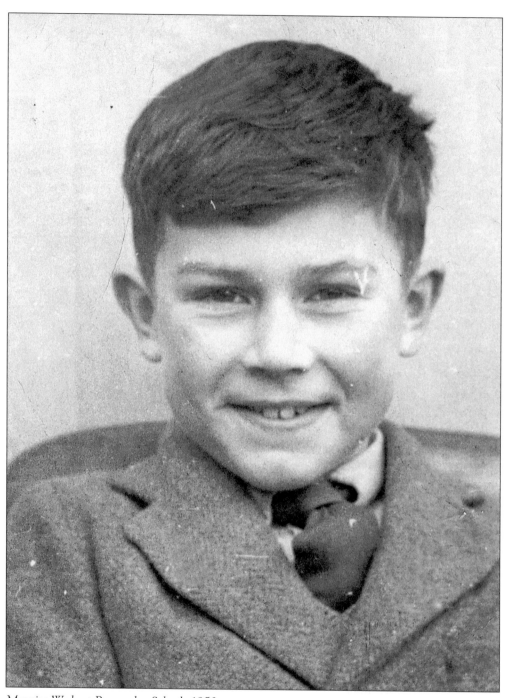

Maurice Wade at Barrowden School, 1950.

when I was at Burley Road School I jumped for the county. Mr Bracegirdle called me up to the stage the next morning to praise me. The next day I got the ruler for running in the corridor!

Christine Baum

Double Desks

When I was at the local school in Barrowden one teacher I remember was Mrs Dixie. She taught the seniors. At one stage there were over a hundred children there, and only two teachers. We sat in double desks in rows in one half of a large room. In the other half it was empty and we went there for assembly, singing, dancing and games. There were two fires in that room and one fire in the infant's room. In the winter it was *so* cold.

Maurice Wade

Across the Fields

I went to Ridlington school for a time. That was about ten minutes walk across the fields or up the lane which in winter time was often muddy and wet. There were times in the winter when we were snowed in.

I had a nervous illness when I was about eight which was caused by a schoolteacher so I then went to Preston school. Preston is a good mile and a half from Ridlington. I was there until I did my eleven plus and then I went to Uppingham Central School. When I first went to school I think I started by writing on a slate. We sat at desks which were rather uncomfortable things. There were two desks together an a long seat with a back attached. You had to sit up straight!

Elsie Rose

Hot Soup

We would walk from Stocken to Stretton for school. In the winter we would take soup and the teacher would heat it up on the stove.

George Goodwin

Cooking the Dinner

I went to Uppingham Central School in September 1931. I had to walk to Ayston and wait to be picked up and taken to the market place at Uppingham. Then there was another mile and a half to walk to the central school which was between Uppingham and Lyddington. The school was in two former prisoner-of-war huts that were used in the First World War. There were three classrooms and two cloakrooms in one, and in the other was the domestic science room and the woodwork room.

We learnt to cook. When the girls reached form two and form three, two of them were chosen each day to cook the dinner for those staying. It was a hot meal and I think they charged 4d. When you cooked the meal you were supervised by the domestic science teacher. We would cook fish and chips, stews, and puddings. The puddings were usually steamed

Richard Wright, one of Geoff Wright's brothers, at Ketton School, 1953.

puddings. We always had to work out the cost of the meals we cooked.

We learned needlework, too. One of the first things I had to make was a pinafore to wear when we did cookery. We had to make the pattern and cut it out. I remember I chopped the hem off mine and the teacher was not very pleased with me! We made our own binding for the neck by cutting the material on the cross into long strips.

Elsie Rose

No Talking

I went to the infants school in Church Street and then to the junior school and then to what was called the Oakham Central School. I didn't like domestic science at the central school. Well, I didn't like the teacher so I did woodwork instead. In those days, the children who came from the villages eat in the same room as we did cookery. So if you had domestic science in the morning, you had to prepare the dinners for the children that day. There was a lady who did the cooking but we had to do the preparing.

We had a third of a pint of milk at school .When we first had it, it was a ha'penny a day. We used to have it about eleven o'clock when we had playtime. The milk came in a crate and there was a milk monitor to give it out. School was very different in those days. We all sat in rows of desks and you weren't allowed to talk in class or walk around. You had to sit still.

Eileen Snow

School Milk

I first went to Ketton school and then on to Casterton. At Ketton, when I first went, the headmaster was Mr Nunn and he must have been headmaster for quite sometime. Then Mr Knowles came and he was a much younger man. We used to have milk there every day. Someone used to come round with a tray with small, shallow glasses with milk in.

When I went to Casterton the bus used to pick us up at eight o'clock in the morning to take us to school. When I was there they had third of a pint bottles of milk for everyone.

Geoff Wright

Force of Personality

I came to Barrowden when I was three weeks old and I went to the village school. The first teacher I had was Miss Harris. I remember the first day at school, which would be in 1935. It was after the Easter break and there was a late winter, early spring snowstorm. I can remember going to school and it snowed like mad. One small girl, whose name was Rita Long, took me by the hand and led me to one of those bottle-type stoves to warm my hands.

I remember trying to learn the alphabet, which was strung along the wall. I vividly remember the letter R. It was R for Rover – and Rover was a sheepdog. I could not get it into my head. All I could think of was dog – R for dog!

When we left the infants class, which was in the little room, we would go up into the big room where there were two fires. It was a long room. Mrs Dixie was the headmistress and she sat at a large desk between the two fires. In that room there was Standard One, Standard Two, Standard Three, Standard Four and Standard Five and they were all in lines. We had to learn our tables.

In the winter, which was always bitterly cold because we seemed to have bitterly cold winters then, chilblains were very prevalent. You had them on your fingers and on your toes. On the very cold days you moved desks every fifteen minutes or so. The front desk got the warmth from the fire, then after quarter of an hour you went to the back. Mrs Dixie, without raising her voice too much, had the force of personality to make the room quiet by looking at every one.

Robin Ellis

In the Stables

When I first went to school it was in the stables at Burley-on-the-Hill, adjacent to the main house. There were two rooms that the Finches had made for a school. We went there when we were five years old and there would be about twenty pupils. All the village children went there – the farm worker's children and the estate worker's children. When I was there my teacher was Mrs Wilder and later there was a Miss Duffin. The school was closed about 1944 and we all went to Cottesmore Junior School. There was a bus laid on but we often biked in the summer.

Ray Hill

Buckets

There were no flush toilets at the school. There were just ordinary buckets with a seat.

Elsie Rose

Coloured Card

From Parkfield Road, there was a path we took to school going near the church in Oakham. It was quite a walk. I used to go to school in the morning and go home for dinner. We finished about quarter past twelve and went back for half past one.

The dentist, Mr Mactaggart, used to come to school with a caravan. We would be given one coloured card to take home and if you had to have something done you were given another one. I was a naughty girl because I hated the dentist. Once I went to Mr Mactaggart and he said he was going to take a tooth out so I got out of the chair and he smacked my bottom. I went back to Miss Strickland's class and she put me near the fire because she thought I'd had this tooth out. All of a sudden there was a knock on the window and it was Mr Mactaggart who told her what I'd done.

Eunice Hill

All Rounders

We played netball in the winter and cricket in the summer. Occasionally, we played rounders.

Elsie Rose

Oakham School CCF Band, c. 1956.

Saturday School

When I went to school in Oakham, I left Barrowden at eight o'clock in the morning to cycle to Luffenham station where we left our bikes and caught the train. Then they put on a bus which stopped at the Halfway House pub in South Luffenham. That was better especially when we used to come back at night. At the grammar school in the two winter terms they had lessons between four o'clock and six o'clock, and sport in the afternoon. We missed the last lesson because we had to catch the train. We would get home at about quarter to seven. We went to school on Saturdays too.

Maurice Wade

Saluting the Flag

On May Day we would have a maypole at Stretton School and also a flagpole. On Empire Day we had to stand and salute the

Oakham School library with headmaster C.G.T. Griffiths.

flag. I think I remember Major Hesketh and the parson would come and watch us.

George Goodwin

Moving Classrooms

When I first went to school it was to the local PNEU School. It was a little school with about twelve children all between five and eight years old. The teacher was Miss Fullerton. The school moved about because it was a primary school for the sons and daughters of Uppingham schoolteachers before they went to boarding school. Some town children went in as well if there was

room. It moved about to different school houses. One year you would be in West Dean and another year you might be in the Hall. It depended on who had children at the school and where there was room available. I went onto Oakham School when I was eight.

I was leaving home about quarter past eight for school and would get home at half past six. On Tuesdays and Thursdays we got home about half past five. Then there was homework. That took an hour and a half to two hours and that included Saturday nights. We used to go to school all day on Saturday, until five o'clock. As I got older I had more chores to do. During the holiday time it was quite busy and I was expected to do a certain amount on the farm.

We used to keep the hens up the field and in the summer time, once I'd got a bicycle when I was eight or nine, it was my job to go and shut the hens up. That was any time from eight to half past nine.

John Tabrum

Rows of Desks

I went to the village school until I was ten when I went to the High School at Stamford. At the village school the headmaster was Mr Lunn. We sat in rows of desks. We used to write with pens that you dipped into the ink. We played bat and ball or spinning tops.

Georgina Andrews

Tin Huts

One teacher I remember was old Mrs Bennett. She came from Oakham. I started school in 1919 and she arrived after me. When I started, the headmaster's name was Mr Roberts but I can only just remember him. We had two teachers and a pupil-teacher who was about sixteen or seventeen, I suppose. When I left there I went to Oakham Central School. It was made up of a lot of tin huts then. They were all army huts that were left over from the First World War. We children used to get the train from Manton to Oakham. Some used to come right from Ryhall, and Casterton. We used to meet the train about quarter to nine and get it back about half past four. It was an early start for them at Ryhall.

I didn't like school very much! In fact,

Wing school children in the 1920s.

The day boys' dining room at Oakham School.

I think it was the happiest day of my life when I left!

Raymond Birch

The Doz

We used to get on our bikes and cycle to Luffenham Station and get the train – which we called The Doz – and which took us to Stamford and then we walked up to the grammar school. It was a 'push-and-pull' train with the engine in the middle between two carriages. It used to run from Stamford to Uppingham so it went Stamford, Ketton, Luffenham, Morcott then Seaton and along a little branch line into Uppingham. It never turned round. It either went backwards or forwards and it was based at Seaton.

We had bitterly cold winters and we would still have to cycle to the station. The engine used to freeze up so they had to light a fire under it to thaw it out. Sometimes the train was very late.

Robin Ellis

Copperplate Writing

The first school I went to was the Church of England school opposite Oakham church.

Opposite the west entrance of the church was the playground and it took over the whole of the corner. Mr Hicks was the headmaster at the time. I remember him well because we were taught to write properly. A series of hooks were drawn on the blackboard and the first lesson was just making hooks with the downstroke which was heavier than the upstroke. The idea was to work towards copperplate writing. Mr Hicks came round and showed us how to hold the pen correctly which you had to do if you wanted good copperplate writing. We had an inkwell in the desk and you dipped the pen into this while you were writing.

We had four 'houses' in this little school. There was Nelson, Raleigh, Livingstone and Gordon, and each 'house' had a different colour. I was the prefect in Gordon. We were given extra time off on a Friday. If you were in the house which had saved the greatest amount in National Savings you were given an extra hour off on the Friday afternoon. We used to buy stamps and put them in a book. We would try and buy one 2s 6d stamp each week and when we'd saved up to a pound's worth we got a certificate.

When we did arithmetic we had to chant the tables. The whole class chanted. After that, if I couldn't remember one, like

Diana Robinson (now Scott) at Home Farm, Auston, in the early days of the Second World War. Note the tape across the windows to stop them shattering if a bomb was dropped nearby.

Ketton School in the 1950s.

nine times eight, I used to chant up to it from the beginning and then it would come back to me. We had to deal with pounds, shillings and pence too.

I got a scholarship to go to Oakham School when I was eleven. In those days there were only about 200 pupils there. I think there were about a dozen scholarships offered then, and that included girls who would go to Stamford High School.

Eddie Butcher

The Misses Masters

I first went to a little private school in Uppingham run by two sisters, the Misses Masters. They had a little room which was

near Tabrum's cow shed. There were about fifteen of us. My sister and I used to walk there and back from Ayston every day.

Di Scott

CHAPTER 3
House and Home

Rowland Hill, the great-grandfather of Raymond Hill, seen outside his home in New Row, Burley, 1911. He was the head wagoner for Ben Painter at Cow Close Farm on Exton Lane. Ben Painter was known to be a breeder of Leicestershire sheep.

Everyone Helped

In the mornings mum used to get up and light the fire. It had a back boiler which heated the water – there was no central heating in those days. We all had jobs to do in the house. You helped polish, clean and shop and you didn't expect anything for doing it either. We had to help fold the sheets on wash day and turn the feather beds. If you didn't turn them regularly they became very lumpy. My mother did all her own decorating and we would help size the paper. They were very fancy papers in the fifties.

Christine Baum

Chopping Wood

One of my jobs at home was chopping wood. I used to do it in the lunch break when I was at the village school. I used to really enjoy it and I used to do it on my own because my brother was six years younger than me. I used to count the pieces. We used to have an hour and three quarters, finishing at twelve and going back at quarter to two. Mind you, you wouldn't get out until four o'clock.

Maurice Wade

Soap and Soda

When I was ten my father married again and I had to start helping my step-mum in the house. I had to wash up and I remember the dinner pots would be waiting for me when I came out of school at four o'clock. We used soap to wash up and soda to get rid of the grease. That made my hands very sore and sometimes they'd bleed. We had a tank to collect rainwater outside but no water was laid on at the house. There was a well and we had a pump in the kitchen.

Monica Leclere

Nothing Wasted

Mum's people had a smallholding in Hambleton and their house was flooded when they made Rutland Water. Father and grandfather had allotments off Burley Road and so we always had plenty of vegetables. Every Sunday we had beef and Yorkshire pudding but we never had the Yorkshire pudding with the meat as we do now. We had it first and then we had meat, potatoes and vegetables. I didn't like gravy so I didn't have it with the Yorkshire pudding. I think chicken was my favourite meal. There were always chickens running around.

Mother belonged to the Women's Institute and she was very good at making jams and pastry. She used to bottle fruit and she would salt down beans and pickle eggs. In our front room we had a cupboard with a big jar of pickled eggs. We had everything on the allotment and nothing was wasted. It was made into jam or preserved. My mother used to make a beautiful blackberry vinegar. You had it on plain steamed pudding which we used to call a boiled light pudding. There was no fruit in it. The blackberry vinegar was also very good because our family would get croup and mother used to get an eggcup, put a drop of it in, a little knob of butter and a drop of warm water and it used to soothe the croup.

We used to store apples on trays under the beds to keep them through the winter.

When I was a girl I used to get chilblains on my toes and my fingers. Mother used to rub cream on then but they were still painful.

Eileen Snow

Overcoats

Sometimes the winters were very cold. We used to have a roaring fire, have a screen round it and sit there with our overcoats on to keep warm.

George Goodwin

Keeping Warm

We had a copper warming pan and my dad used to go up and warm our beds with that in winter when it was very cold. He used to take the coals off the fire and put them in the pan. Then we had old stone hot water bottles that we put in the beds.

When it was cold I wore knitted dresses that an aunt used to make for me. I wore navy bloomers, thick black stockings, a liberty bodice and combinations! Then I had different petticoats. I wore button boots and I had a button hooker and gloves and a muff. On my head I wore a bonnet or a woolly hat.

Monica Leclere

Keeping a Pig

We kept a pig in a sty at the end of the garden. My parents had a window that was taken out of the house so they put it in the pigsty! We also kept chickens. The garden provided pretty well everything we needed. When we killed the pig we had the meat. The hams were laid out on trays and salted. That was something I think the butcher did. When the pig was killed, your neighbour would come in and help you sort it all out because some of it had to be distributed straight away. I think they called it pig's fry. It was a great event getting the pig down to the slaughterhouse because it knew what was going to happen!

Maurice Wade

A Routine

We moved to live in Digby Drive, Oakham when we got married and I lived there for forty-seven years. It was a lovely house with a sitting room and double doors leading to the dining room. I did all the decorating – the ceiling, walls and everything. At first I used distemper but it was powdery and would rub off on your clothes, so when they brought out emulsion paint, it was much better and I used that. The colours were beautiful but it wasn't so quick drying.

I used to have a routine; I did the washing on Monday, the ironing on Tuesday, went to see my mother on Wednesday, on Thursday I cleaned all through and on Friday I went to the shops. There wasn't much spare time but when I did have some I used to do sewing and embroidery. I used to make my daughter, Carol's, evening dresses when she was growing up and going to dances. She was a little monkey though, because she would only wear them once or twice and then she'd want a new one!

Anne Spencer

Cleaning Knives

On a Saturday morning we had to clean the knives. They were made of steel but not stainless steel in those days. If anything acid like vinegar touched the knives, that stained them so when you washed them up you rubbed them with a sort of pumice stone which fetched some of it off. When we cleaned them on Saturdays we used Bathbrick. We dipped a piece of steel wool in the Bathbrick and rubbed the blades. It was hard work.

We had a sink at home but Joe's mother in Milner's Row. There was a bath with all the washing in and that was done on the kitchen table. They had an open fire with no boiler and no copper and every drop of water had to be hotted on the fire. She would put a sheet in the big, iron, oval pot of water on the fire, one at a time, to boil them clean. That was the only way she could do it. She added Hudson's powder which was in little yellow packets and that was good because it would fetch stains and marks out. Then there was Preservine soap which had to be sliced up and put in the pot. That had a nice smell.

You always used soda in the water to get rid of the grease. It didn't do your hands much good. I've seen Joe's mum with great big cracks down the side of her thumbs. Washing was real hard work. She had to do the boiler suits which were oily because Joe and his dad worked in the foundry, and I've seen the perspiration dripping off her nose in the summer. How she lived like that, with eight children, I don't know.

May Wright

Bottom Drawer

I was engaged for two years before we married and I kept a 'bottom drawer'. I collected a lot of things for the house and I sewed for it.

Georgina Andrews

Killing the Badger

My sister, Dorothy and I took it in turns fetching the milk before we went to school in the morning. We had a tin can with a top on that held about two pints and we used to go across the village green to Miss Lane, the farmer. There was a brass knocker on the door and it's still there today. When we got back from school in the afternoon we'd go again.

In the old days the toilets were in little brick places in the garden. They were round, tin buckets with a handle that folded down and they were under a wooden box with a hole in. Every so often you had to empty them so you would dig a hole in the garden to empty it. When anybody said they were going to kill the badger, you knew they were going to empty the bucket.

Ray Hill

The Cross Keys

I was born in The Cross Keys in New Street which was pulled down when the supermarket was built. My mother and father, Lily and Albert Butcher ran The Cross Keys. Before that it was owned by my uncle, Artie Green. One of his sons kept The Horse and Jockey at Manton.

Eddie Butcher

Keeping Food

We grew vegetables and fruit in the garden. There were gooseberries which my mother made into jam and we had a whole row of damson trees. There were also some apple trees. We stored the apples in a shed in the garden. We had to be sure that there

Ray Hill's parents, George and Alice (née Lown), outside their house in Burley.

were no bruises on the apples. Potatoes were stored in a very big tub. At the back of the Lodge there was an old back kitchen and we stored food for winter in there. My mother would make jam and raspberry vinegar and blackberry vinegar.

Elsie Rose

Pumping the Water

In our house in Barrowden there were two bedrooms and a very large landing where you could put at least one bed and possibly two single ones. In about 1949 my parents had the loft converted into a bedroom and a bathroom. We had to pump up the hot water from the wash house, which was next to the house, if you wanted a bath. I think we must have also used the soft water that we collected in a large tank outside the kitchen window. Somehow that was fed into the cold tap. In the wash house, the boiler was in the corner with a fire underneath. There was the mangle kept in there and a dolly for doing the washing. We kept the paraffin there, that was delivered by lorry. The privy was next to the wash house and then there was the pen for the chickens. The pig was at the bottom of the garden. We had a piglet every year that we fattened up. Right across the top of the house was the attic where we stored the apples and the pears ready for eating in the winter. We laid newspaper on the floor and spaced the apples out so they didn't touch. My mother had one of the first calor gas cookers in the village.

Maurice Wade

Mangle Versus Wringer

In those days when you did the washing up, a lot of people used a big washing up bowl on the table with a tray. Not every house had a sink in the kitchen, or water from a tap either. When you did the washing in a tub with a dolly, you had to put it through the wringer or the mangle. I had a wringer. The mangle was a big wooden roller and the wringer had smaller rubber rollers.

Lucy Wiggington

A Good Stew

It would take me all morning to cook a good stew.

Anne Spencer

Helping Mum

We lived in a tied cottage because my dad was horseman to Mr Peasgood, the farmer at Empingham. He worked there for thirty-eight years until he died. If you had a tied cottage that meant that if you left the job you had to leave the cottage. It was a big house. My mum had a lovely big, back scullery with a copper on the side. After I moved to Ryhall I used to cycle back to Empingham one day a week to help my mum do her cleaning. On a nice bicycle with a three-speed it took me about half an hour to do the five and a half miles.

May Wright

The Sunday Roast

On Sunday we always had a roast joint. On a Monday, which was wash day, we would have the joint cold with bubble and squeak. On Tuesday, if there was anything left, it would be minced up. We had sausages sometimes and rice pudding or treacle sponge. When we were kids, chickens were a rarity. I liked mince and liver and gravy. Someone used to come round selling wet fish and we'd have smoked haddock poached in milk.

Geoff Wright

Bath Night

Bath night was a night, I tell you! I had to go round the front of the house and get two buckets of water and then take them round to the wash house and pour them into the copper. I'd heat it up and when it was hot I would cart it into the house and pour it into the old tin bath in front of the fire. We would all have our baths in that one lot of water. I think Kitty and I had the first ones and then parents. Afterwards I had to take the water in buckets back down to the wash house and tip it down the drain. You only had a bath once a week in those days!

George Goodwin

Lasting All Winter

We had an allotment and a higgledy-piggledy garden. In the front garden we grew roses. We grew beetroot, broad beans, runner beans, and potatoes at the back. I had six hundredweight of potatoes, one time! We dug a hole and put potatoes and swedes in and they lasted all winter.

Anne Spencer

Growing Fruit

In most ways we were self-sufficient. In the garden we grew red currants, black currents, gooseberries, loganberries, and raspberries. There were apple and plum trees.

Maurice Wade

Everyone Had a Job

We were quite a big family and we all had jobs to do. One of my jobs at night was to scrape all the new potatoes ready for the next day's dinner. My brothers had to chop sticks for the fire and get the coal in. Every Thursday night my sister had to clean the pantry out and wipe all the shelves down. We couldn't go out to play until we had done the jobs. I had a paper round when I was about ten or eleven. I went out at seven o'clock and after I'd done the round I used to have to call at the greengrocer's for potatoes or at the butcher's for some meat for dinner to take home. Mum used to give me a list.

Eunice Hill

No Central Heating

We always had a pig and we used to hang the hams up in the kitchen. Monday was wash day, whatever happened. And then Tuesday was ironing day. My mother had a tub with a dolly or she would wash by hand. We would air the sheets by hanging them outside in the sunshine.

Winters were bitterly cold here because we had no central heating. My father always got up and lit the fire first thing in the morning. He used to take the ashes out the back in a dustpan. We always had a good breakfast – egg and bacon. My father worked in Stamford at Arthur Lyons.

Georgina Andrews

Using a Flat Iron

My mother used to make lovely rabbit stews and bread pudding. I used to love it cold. She made big Roly Poly puddings which she boiled in cloths in black pots. They had jam in them. If they had currents in then they were called Spotted Dicks. She also made lovely apple dumplings. Dad used to grow all his vegetables and we had hens at the top of the garden.

It used to take my mother two days to do the washing and then she had all the ironing to do. She had a dolly tub and a bath with the blue in. The starch was in another bath. We had to fill the copper and light it underneath and she would do all the boiling in that. It was hard work. We helped fold the sheets and pull them straight and then we had to hold them while she put them through the wooden mangle to press them. She used flat irons which she heated on the range. She used two so while she was using one the other one was heating up.

Eunice Hill

First Light the Fire

Father used to get up early and the first job he did was light the fire to get the house warm. We used to have a cooked breakfast every morning – fried bread, fried egg, tomatoes, sausage, bacon. I remember sitting at the table and eating this big breakfast, particularly when I went to school in Oakham. That was in 1950.

Maurice Wade

Bacon and Eggs

My sister Florrie Dolby who lived in Exton, kept a pig. I used to take her eggs and she brought me bacon!

May Wright

Next Door Neighbours

When we were first married we lived next door to my parents. In those days we couldn't afford a wireless set. Mother had one so we had the wires through to our bungalow and had a loudspeaker. Kitty could talk into it and mother could answer her!

We had a dartboard at home and Kitty

used to play the insurance man round the board at darts. She used to play him for a penny to win. We also had a Devil among the Tailors or skittles with a ball on the string.

George Goodwin

No Name

I was born in the first house up the hill in Aldgate. It didn't have a name but everyone knew that was where the Scotchbrooks lived. I lived in Ketton until I was sixteen and then I went to London where I trained as a children's nurse in Putney. I came home here when I was twenty-five and I married a Ketton lad. He was the butcher's son. The butcher, Eddie Andrews, was also a farmer. The farm we have now was his farm. The shop was at the crossroads. When we were first married we lived down Bull lane. This farm was land that belonged to Mr Burroughs and it was a fruit farm and my husband's father bought it from him.

Georgina Andrews

Everybody Did It

I spent the early years of my life in Ketton. I was actually born at No. 47 High Street and we lived in No. 45 where we were until 1957 and then we moved to No. 35.

I always helped father potato picking. We used to get the potatoes and dry them in the back yard. We'd sort them out and only bag up the better ones for storage. The ones that were badly bruised or had a fork stuck in them we'd use up straight away. Only the best

were kept.

We had a cellar at No. 45 and the coal and wood were kept down there. I sometimes chopped the sticks on the cellar steps which was a firm base. Numbers 40, 43, 45 and 47 had cellars.

We had no garden at home so father had an allotment in Pit Lane. They were the Whiteread Allotments which I think was the name of a Trust. There were allotments all over in Ketton. Some were by the railway between Mill Dam and the Barrowden Road, some were round Aldgate. The Luffenham Road council houses and Highfield estate had big gardens. We used a clamping system to keep vegetables, especially potatoes. Everybody used to do it. You dig a hole in the ground, lay straw in it and put the vegetables in, cover them with straw, and then the soil you had dug out to make the hole you put on top of the straw. You did that with carrots, beetroot, potatoes – all root vegetables. Farmers did that, years ago. Potatoes lasted fairly well through the year and there were greens, carrots and swedes and parsnips over the winter.

Geoff Wright

Feeding the Pigs

My father kept a few pigs and one of my jobs was to mash up all the household food waste into pig's swill and feed the pigs. We had no electricity in the house when I was a boy. It may have been put in downstairs just before the war, but it was after the war before it was put upstairs. We used candles and paraffin lamps.

Robin Ellis

Salt Beef

When I was a lad we always had meat to eat, well, we lived next door to the butcher. I like salt beef sandwiches. My mother used to do it herself. It was meat that couldn't be sold in the joint – ends, pieces with a bit of fat on. She would cook it and then when it was done, put it in a pot with a heavy brick on top of it to make it solid.

Raymond Birch

Nipping Out to Watch Telly

We had a telly at home. It had a great big cabinet and a very tiny screen and it was black and white. My grandparents Stafford had a television before we did and because Bull Lane where they lived was just round the corner from us, on a Saturday night we used to get washed and ready for bed in slippers and dressing gown and then nip round to watch their telly. There was 'Saturday Night Out' and 'The Billy Cotton Band Show' that I remember watching. Then eventually my father bought a television of our own.

Geoff Wright

CHAPTER 4
Games We Played

Wakeley and Barrowden Cricket team in the early 1950s. From left to right, back row: Walter Perry (scorer), Cecil Dolby, Arthur Pridmore, Alec Roberts, George Cole, Hughie Cole. Middle row: George Roberts, Les Simms, Charlie Gilman. Front row: George Mason, Jim Hopkins, Charlie Barfield.

Hollering

We used to play with a whip and top. That was a stick with a leather bootlace tied to it and a knot at the end. We would make our own tops using a stud from a hobnail boot. You would wind the bootlace round and flick it and see how far it would spin away. We also had hoops. There were often old cycles thrown into the hedges by the troops stationed at north Luffenham. We would get these and take the spokes out of the wheels to make hoops.

The winters always seemed very hard and

we used to go sledging. We made our sledges from slats of wood. I used to cut through the bicycle wheel rims and straighten them out and they would make lovely runners for the edges.

You could roam all over the fields. Alfie Colston, Gethlin Johnson, Noel Shelvey lived at Morcot across the fields. We used to whistle especially if it was foggy or dark so we wouldn't miss each other. We all had a different sounding whistle so you could tell who was coming. But if you thought someone was a long way away we used to shout, or what we would call, 'holler'. You would put your hands around your mouth and holler as loud as you could. Then if you heard someone else holler back, you would home into it. You could tell by the holler who it was and as soon as you heard it you'd holler back their names.

When we got together we used to go to the Boot and Shoe pub at South Luffenham which was also a bake house. The baker was called Charlie Palfreyman and he was the most incredible baker. My old mate Alfie Colston liked the middle of the bread and I liked the crust. We were a good combination! For a shilling we would get a loaf of bread for fourpence ha'penny and a bottle of pop for sixpence ha'penny so we had a penny left. We would drink so much of the pop and keep filling up the bottle from the spring. We used to get pop from the Halfway House on the top road. In those days you could get a ha'penny back on a bottle if it had a sticker on it. We found where there were bottles dumped and Mike Sismey, whose dad kept The Boot and Shoe, said he could get the stickers to put on them then we could take them back to the pub for the ha'penny!

We used to go scrumping, too. There were some lovely orchards around and one in particular belonged to a Charlie Hall. Before we went scrumping we used to plan it. We always said that if anyone saw us we were to run up the Barrowden road so they'd think we were Barrowden boys. You'd always carry a piece of string when you went scrumping and you'd tie this round your waist so that you could stuff the apples down the front of your shirt and they wouldn't fall out at the bottom.

Alan Fox

Tickling Trout

Down the bottom of Mill lane there was a stream going across the road and there was always trout in that stream. Walter Barwell and I used to tickle trout. We used to go in the osier bushes and find bird's nests. There were some down Mill lane and some at the top.

Arthur Branson

Wooden and iron

When I was very young we played with tops in the street. We had a whip and you wound it round the little top and got it spinning and then you whipped it to keep it going. We also played with hoops. There were wooden ones which didn't last long and there were iron ones.

Eddie Butcher

Football and Cricket

I learnt to play cricket on the village green at Barrowden. There was a very good team in my day that won everything. There were people in it like Alf Roberts and his older brother George, and Arthur Trimble (I think) from Wakeley and they used to do the bowling. From Barrowden there was Cliff Baines, Hughie Cole and his brother George. They were the bakers. I used to go with Hughie on a Saturday and help deliver bread at Wakeley, Fineshade and Laxton. Jim Hopkin was another cricketer, and Les Peasgood, Charlie Gilman and Dr Wallis. These were my boyhood heroes.

I used to go on practice nights – Tuesdays and Fridays – and they would have a net put up. In my day they played by the river on the meadows which was between the old railway and the river. The young lads played on the village green with a soft ball. As lads we played football on the recreation ground in the winter.

Maurice Wade

Shooting

As a boy we always had air guns and did a bit of shooting in the stack yard next door. There was me and my brother, Bob, Jimmy Carter and John Tyler, the farmer's grandson. I was just a bit older, we were always together. There was one time when I was walking back home and I couldn't find any sparrows to shoot. The man who kept the Cuckoo, Mr Adnitt, had some poultry and the gates were always open so they were always across the road. I took a shot at the cock and I must have hit it straight in the head because it dropped down dead. There were some bushes down the bottom of the stack yard so I ran with it down there. Nobody ever knew!

Raymond Birch

Cigarette Cards

When we were at school we used to play with marbles and hoops. We had hoops which we bowled along with a stick. When we got more money we had a steel one with a ring round it. We also used to play with cigarette cards. We would flick them up against a wall and if your opponent flicked his on top of yours, then he took them both

George Goodwin

Hopscotch

We used to play in the street. There was a circle at the top of Parkfield Road and we all used to play in there. We would tie a string to the lamp post to act as a maypole. Sometimes we'd play hopscotch and skipping. There were skipping games we played like 'one, two, three, alara, I saw sister Sarah ...' We used to swing the rope low and then jump over it and turn it so the others could run through it. Sometimes we had a rope in each hand with one turning one way and the other the opposite way.

Eunice Hill

A young Geoff Wright fishing at Wash Dyke on the River Chater in Ketton.

Jumping the Hedges

We would run across the fields to Clipsham, which was about a mile or so away, and jump over the hedges because they were only low.

George Goodwin

Bladders

We played football and during the war we had bladders in the balls. When they burst you couldn't get any more so you stuffed the balls with paper. When we played cricket, if the bat broke we used a piece of wood.

Robin Ellis

Weed Fights

I used to go off fishing on my own in the Chater or the Welland. There was no particular spot and I varied where I went. There were odd times when I'd go with John Phillips and in our teenage years we did a fair bit of fishing together. We'd catch roach, chub and eel. We did quite a bit of eel fishing because eel was something we could catch and know that people would eat. At odd times my eldest brother Richard would come fishing with me or we'd go down the river messing about with other people. We'd end up having a weed fight and coming home plastered in green weeds and getting a good hiding!

Geoff Wright

Cricket in the Field

We had skipping tops and hoops and we played hopscotch and skipping. We played rounders outside. There was a field at the back of the blacksmith's shop where we used to play cricket. My dad's uncle lived next door to us and he had a smallholding and he let us go in the field. His name was Joe Wright, and when he moved the people who took over still let us play there. We used to have loads of snow in winter so we would toboggan on fields that we called The Banks and The Dog Well.

We used to go for long walks in the fields and sometimes we'd play Fox and Hounds. One ran off and they'd leave a trail and after a while the others would try and follow it. We played Hide and Seek, too.

Monica Leclere

Conkers

We played conkers. You'd put a conker on a string by making a hole with a skewer, threading the string through and tying a knot at the end. When you played you had three goes at your opponent's conker to try and break it and if you didn't break it then he had a go at yours. Whoever ended up with a whole conker was the winner. We used to try and find the biggest one and sometimes we'd pop it in the oven to make it a little bit harder!

Ray Hill

No Cars

Along the Burley road there was a path and a pipe, a gas pipe I think it was, that came up out of the ground and then went across the path and shut it off. We used to tipple over it and it was called The Tipples, you know, summersault. In the park there use to be some bars we could climb up and do acrobatics. We used to have some good fun. There weren't any cars whizzing up and down the street. There were seasons for games. We played tops along the street and hoops and ball games. We did skipping most of the year round. In winter it was mostly with hoops. In the summer we down to the park.

In Cutts Close in Oakham, they had a man who used to scythe the grass. We used to get the grass that he'd scythed and pile it up and make little houses. We would make different rooms in the houses. Mother would give us sandwiches in a little basket to take down there. Sometimes she'd give us home-made lemonade in a bottle. We'd usually see granddad there because it was his job to look after Cutts Close. He used to lock the swings up at half past five every night, and the same with the see-saws. The chain would be over the bottom bit.

When I was ten, Oakham School let the swimming baths to the council for the summer. We learnt to swim there. I used to go swimming down the canal before that. There was a diving board at the school. We would go morning, noon and night to the school. The water was cold and it was very basic. There was a bit of sacking up for us to change behind.

Eileen Snow

Cowboys and Indians

We played Cowboys and Indians. We wore old trousers with a bit of fur round the bottom as the cowboys and we'd try and get a band to put round our heads and stick a feather in it when we were Indians. We used to play that in Burley wood. There was Reg Grimmer, David Healey, John Lane, and some of the young boys who lived round the corner – Dennis, John, Bernard, Kenny and Michael. Every lunchtime, the eldest one, Bernard, would come outside and call each one separately for dinner.

There were plenty of soldiers around when I was a boy and we used to try and copy them. We used to dig a trench and get in it and they'd be throwing bricks and stones at us. One night I was hit on the head and I had a red handkerchief. When I got home to mother she thought the handkerchief was soaked with blood. There was a bit of blood but not nearly as much as she thought!

Ray Hill

Ghost Train

I didn't have a lot of time to play games, other than organized games. We played rugby, cricket or hockey at Oakham School three or four days a week, there was CCF Corp one or two days a week in the afternoon so there was not a lot of time. The friends I had were mostly kids I'd known at PNEU. They were very lucky because living in the school houses they had huge gardens. You could play cricket on the lawns for days on end in the summer. You'd make dens in the spinney at the bottom of the garden. One year in Constable House, during the Christmas holidays, we built a ghost train round the boys' dining hall. It took us about three days to build. We turned the tables onto their edges, which formed a sort of a channel, and we had a little cart in which we sat people (the parents were the victims) so they couldn't see over the top of the tables and pulled them around. Then we flashed lights and had things that sparked and boomed and we waved material in front. Sometimes we'd get all our electric train sets and join them together and spread them out all over the floor so you had a huge layout. We made our own entertainment. There was no television. We had our first one in time to watch the Coronation in 1953.

John Tabrum

Pinching Petrol

Robert Hassell used to live up at the top of Pit Lane in Ketton. The pair of us tried to build an underground den in the woods behind his house. That was hard work. We got the hole dug and then started looking

North Luffenham Cricket team in the 1930s. Arthur Branson is seated 3rd from the right.

for timber to put on the roof and lost interest.

In the late fifties or early sixties, we had a trolley and we put a little Mobillette engine on the back wheel. To get petrol, we used to go and pinch it out of the cricket club mower or we'd go round the building site at Ketton, picking the Corona bottles up, taking them back to the shop and getting 3d on each one. Then we could go and buy the petrol.

Geoff Wright

CHAPTER 5
Off to Work

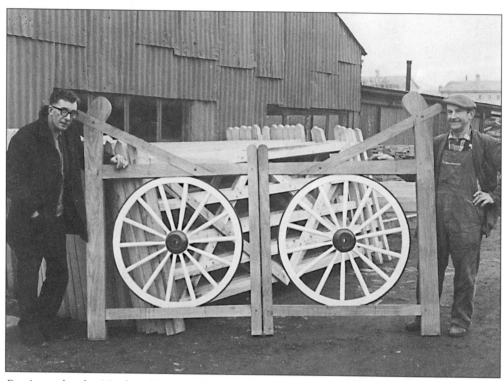

Rose's woodyard in North Luffenham. Alan Rose (left) and Arthur Branson with a pair of gates made by the firm.

Turning a Hand

When I worked for Alan Rose at North Luffenham we used to make sheep's troughs, cattle cribs and horse mangers. We used to make gates as well. We made a lovely pair of gates and they stood in the wood yard until they went rotten because the man who ordered them never collected them. I could turn my hand to most things. I started working for Roses in Normanton Park. When he set me on he knew who I was because he talked about my granddad, William Branson, who used to ride a donkey. We made gateposts and pit props for the mines with little pieces, four by two,

TO ALL AGRICULTURAL LABOURERS.

A Message from the Prime Minister.

I ask all workers on the land to do their very utmost to help to grow more food.

There is a shortage of food all over the world, and we may have to feed our Army and Navy, as well as ourselves, on what we can grow at home. They cannot fight on unless they are properly fed.

Every full day's work that you do helps to shorten the war, and brings peace and victory nearer.

Every idle day and all loitering lengthen the war and lessen the chance of victory.

Your Comrades in the trenches are under fire every hour of the day and night. Will you not help them to win by working an extra hour each day ?

That is. the way in which you can beat the Germans !

January 1, 1918.

Lloyd George

(1629) . G 460 . 250,000 . 1/18 . J. T. & S., Ltd. 162.

A message from the Prime Minister.

called caps to go on the tops. Some of the better wood went to London for veneers.

At the woodyard, there were great big engines that were made by Blackstone's in Stamford and they used to keep the saws going. An engine had to have six water tanks to keep it cool. When it was working, on a clear day you could hear the sawmill at Empingham. One of my jobs was to heat the oil to start the engine. We used to get timber from all round the area. A lot of it came from Lord Ancaster's estate. We sometimes went to Holme Fen near Peterborough.

Arthur Branson

Six Mile Walk

I left school at fourteen. I wanted to go into nursing but I didn't have the qualifications so I went to a small shop in Uppingham called the Ranksborough Dairy. I had to be there by nine in the morning and one of my jobs was to deliver some milk and I would tidy the shop. I spent about a year there. I still had to walk there and back which was a good six miles a day. In the winter it was dark when I walked home. Never ever was I afraid to walk alone. In those days you were perfectly safe even though it was a lonely road.

Elsie Rose

Frozen Fish

My father, Frank Ellis, had an uncle who kept a fish and chip shop and he had a brainwave to bring fish and chips to the people in the villages. He had an old Rover car, took the body off and with the aid of a local carpenter put an old hut on in its place. Then he found a kitchen range and put that inside. Coming up to the war I used to go round with him on a Saturday morning. He made enough money to have a purpose-built van on an old Ford model T and in 1938 he had a really smart van made. He had a little Ford car and he used to meet the twenty minutes to eight train from Peterborough every morning at Wakeley station. On it was a wooden box packed with ice and full of frozen fish. The old box was put on the train to go back to the suppliers who were Snowdens of Grimsby. He used to set off with the fish and chip van at about four o'clock in the afternoon and he would not get back home until nearly midnight. He always had an assistant but they didn't last that long.

Robin Ellis

Nursery maid

I came to work for the Chesterman's in Wing as a nursery maid to two little girls, Gilly and Ann. There was a nanny, too. My job was to give them their meals and tidy and clean the bedrooms. I wore a cap and apron. In the mornings it used to be a striped linen dress with a white apron that had straps over the back. In the afternoon, I would have a black dress with a cap and apron.

There were five of us all together – a cook and a kitchen maid, the two of us and a parlour maid. I was also an under-housemaid and had to clean the fires out in the mornings. We had one half day off a week

Frank Ellis's original fish and chip van in 1929, which visited thirty villages every week.

and every other Sunday when I went home to Preston on my bicycle. I was there for six years until I married in 1938. There was not enough room for the five of us to live in the house so we slept in the cottage on the top street.

Gladys Birch

Choices

When I left school at fourteen, Major Hesketh sent for me and I had to go up to the Hall. He gave me an option. I could either go into the Hall and start as a boot boy and work my way up to become a butler, or I could go to the Ram Jam garage and start as an apprentice mechanic. I decided to be a mechanic.

Major Hesketh owned the Ram Jam and he built the garage there. Originally the Ram Jam inn was called the Winchelsea Arms. When I first started at the garage I did all the dirty jobs. When they dismantled an engine, I was the one that had to clean it. I met some interesting people there when I was serving on the pumps. I can remember meeting Phil Scott the boxer and Malcolm Campbell and his two children.

When the garage closed I heard of a job going at RAF Cottesmore for a fitter. I went for an interview on my motorbike and took Kitty with me in the sidecar. They gave me the job and said they would pay me £5 a week and I would finish work at eleven in the morning on a Saturday! That was in 1939. I worked on anything mechanical – but not the aeroplanes! It was anything that didn't belong to the

George Goodwin greasing Major Hesketh's Rolls Royce at the Ram Jam garage.

The Ram Jam garage and inn taken, 1928. Note the telephone poles!

RAF. When I was made a foreman I was allowed to become a member of the sergeant's mess.

George Goodwin

A White Enamel Can

I came to Whissendine because I was in domestic service and I came to the Red House to work. That must be sixty-eight years ago and four years before I married. I came as a housemaid to Colonel and Mrs Alexander. Mrs Alexander had a staff of four – a cook, a kitchen maid, a parlour maid and me. My jobs were to clean for them and make the beds. I had to see to the wash stands and the chamber pots in the bedrooms. I used a dustpan and brush and polish and cream. In those days, I remember, we used Mansion polish and Vim.

I used to get up about seven ready to start work. It was earlier when they went hunting or cubbing. I used to get up about six then. My first job was to clean out the grates and to do the drawing room, then the stairs and then the landing. I had to use a dustpan and brush mostly but I did have a carpet sweeper. I had to scrub the front door step, but I didn't mind that.

I used to take hot water up to the bedrooms in the morning. The water was put in a white enamel can, which probably held about two pints. I had to put the can in the washbasin and cover it with a towel to keep it warm for when they got up. I would take a tray with cups and saucers and tea and I used to call them at eight. The Colonel had his own bedroom next to his wife's and I think the parlour maid called him. I took the tray in to Mrs Alexander. When they were downstairs having their breakfast then we would be up stripping the beds. We changed the sheets once a week and sent

The breakdown recovery vehicle adapted from a car which was used by the Ram Jam garage.

the sheets to the laundry. When the parlour maid was off duty I did her work as well as my own. Sometimes I used to wash up the tea things out in the servant's hall.

We used to get half a day off a week, and every other Sunday. But in the afternoon when you had done your work you could sit down and read or do some knitting. You didn't sit down very long. Sometimes, if they had any guests I would help wait at table. At night, I had to turn the beds down before they went to bed and lay out their night things ready for them. If it was very cold there was a fire laid in the grate in the bedroom. There was no other heating apart from fires but we didn't take much notice of the cold.

We wore a striped dress or a plain dress of a morning with a big apron. In the afternoon we wore a black dress and a small apron. And we wore a cap, black shoes and black stockings. At night we used to go to bed about ten unless there was a dance on.

Colonel Alexander used to hunt and sometimes the Cottesmore Hunt would meet on the village green and we could see them from the house. There was a lot of excitement then.

Lucy Wiggington

Garden Boy

I started as a garden boy at The Grange in Wing when I was fourteen. I was there for seven years and I got a pound a week. The Grange was owned in those days by Miss Brocklebank and there were just two of us working on the gardens. There was no greenhouse so we used to use horse manure to heat the frames. The seed was put in boxes and into the cold frames, which were put on top of a pile of manure. When it started to rot we would dig out the middle and put some more in.

Miss Brocklebank bought the Grange in 1913. I left the Grange when I was twenty-one, I went to work on the farm and then, in 1940, I started work for the Agriculture

Committee and I was there for twelve years. I was a tractor driver and worked with the thrashing tackle. I think I must have worked on most farms in the county. When you'd finished at one farm you went on to the next. They needed some thrashing after harvest. It was put all in sacks and afterwards the gleaners used to come. Our committee was based at Oakham and it was closed about six months after I finished with it in 1951.

Raymond Birch

Keeping Poultry

We used to keep poultry and when the war broke out we had over 200 chickens. We had a piece of ground over the wall here, and then we had two arks in a field next to the Tally Ho. We used to hatch little white Aylesbury ducklings and we would try and hatch them so they were ready for Bourne market on a Thursday. We'd collect shoe boxes, cut holes in the top and put half a dozen ducklings in each one. I would go down to the corner to catch the bus for Bourne to put them on the market. I'd wait until they were all sold and then I would catch the bus back after dinner in the afternoon with the cash!

We would go round the farmers to sell us pig potatoes, the little ones they didn't want. Then we'd boil them and mash them all up and we used those to feed the poultry.

May Wright

An old threshing machine.

Washing the Pots

I started working at Burley Gardens after I left school at fifteen. They belonged to Colonel Hanbury and in those days he had five gardeners working for him. Being the boy, I had to start at the bottom, mostly washing the pots. There was a special copper to do them in. I also had to help sterilise the soil and it was a job sometimes to get the steriliser going first thing in the morning. It was like a square tank with a fire at the bottom and about three inches of water above it. There was a plate with holes through and then a sort of upturned gutter on the top so the steam came out the sides and through the soil. It killed all the wheat seed and any disease. I also had to deliver the vegetables and fruit to the hospital.

I had to start work at half past seven and finished at five. On a Saturday we finished at twelve. I worked there until I was eighteen and then I had to go and register for National Service at The Lodge in Oakham.

Ray Hill

Doing as Your Mum Tells You

When I left school I went to work at Cora's. I was a tabber but I could have been a flatlocker except I was a bit frightened of the machines. A tabber is someone who sews the tabs on the clothes and a flatlocker is someone who stitches around the vests at the neck. I didn't like factory work and I didn't want to go there but in those days you had to do as your mum told you. Years ago when you left school, you either had to go in service or work in a factory or shop. One of my teachers, Miss Jackson, married the school doctor and she wanted me to go in service for her but my mum wanted me to work at Cora's.

When I married Ray I helped him and his dad in the gardens. I loved doing that. I did the pricking out and the potting, I cut the chrysanths and I did the disbudding.

Eunice Hill

Five Years Apprenticeship

When I left school I went to work in a dress shop, Drusille's, in the High Street in Oakham. It was really a ladies outfitter and they sold everything from corsets to hats.

I was apprenticed after that to the tailor at Furley & Hassan. That would be in 1939. You were apprenticed for five years and I got four shillings a week. It was a big building then. The men's department was where the Imperial Cancer Charity shop is now, and upstairs there was a millinery department, because they made their own hats, a dressmaking department and a tailoring department.

I was there in the tailoring department for ten years and when I left I was earning two pounds, seventeen shillings and six pence. We worked for exactly forty-eight hours a week and that included Saturday mornings. I had to be there at eight o'clock. That meant I earned a penny an hour and if I worked overtime I got a penny-farthing. There were a lot of us in the tailoring room. There was the cutter, Mr Nevison who was in charge and there was a man who was the trimmer. He brought the materials up for the linings. We had to mark out the pattern with chalk ready for cutting. We were three storeys up in the building. We had to go in through the Burley Road entrance, through the garden, round past the washbasins and through a door, up two flights of stairs and then we could leave our coats. Then we went up some steps, through the blanket room, through another door, down a few steps, up some more and we were in the tailoring room! We weren't allowed to go through the shop.

Where the prison is now on the Ashwell Road there used to be an army camp. I had to go down there and help sew on the badges. We used to make officers' uniforms. When the Yanks came we made their new outfits. I used to make the hats to wear with them.

Furley & Hassan was a big department store. They used to serve all the gentry who came up for the hunting. When the war came, things changed.

Eileen Snow

Becoming Self-Employed

My dad, George Hill and I were working for Colonel Hanbury at Burley-on-the-Hill and in 1967 the Labour Government brought out a selective employment tax which meant all the gentry had to pay a tax on chauffeurs, keepers, butlers, gardeners, etc. The agent at the time said to us that it might be a good idea if my dad and I were self-employed. He said, give it a twelve months trial and if it doesn't work out you can come back and work for the Colonel.

So we set up a market garden on two acres of land which had greenhouses that we rented at a very low rent and that included a cottage for me. It used to be the kitchen garden to the big house. The Colonel gave dad his cottage next door rent and rates free, for as long as he lived as a kind of pension because he had worked for him for over fifty years.

We got in touch with Leicester Wholesale Market and we started growing for them but we did sell a few things to Colonel Hanbury. We found it was best to grow flowers and pot plants. We couldn't compete with the Fen growers because they were all mechanized. Being a small area on the side of a hill, we found that if we grew flowers and pot plants it was mainly hand labour so we could compete a bit then. The problem was, after we had started in 1967, we got decimalization, there was the energy crisis, and all costs were going up. The fuel costs especially went up. A load of anthracite would be £250 when we started but by the time we finished it was about £2,000. We worked in Burley Gardens as they were called, until 1990 when Asil Nadir came along and bought the mansion for a hotel and leisure complex. But things went wrong and eventually the architect, Kit Martin, converted it to apartments.

It was good when we did it but we were happy to see it go when the offer was made on the mansion. We used to do seven days a week because it's what you put into it that counts. If you enjoy doing something, you don't notice the hours you put in. When dad passed on it wasn't quite the same. We all pulled together and we were all working for one another. Dad and I, between us, spent over one hundred years working for the Estate. Dad did over sixty-five years.

Ray Hill

CHAPTER 6

High Days and Holidays

Joy O'Shaughnessy (née Wright) aged ten, is crowned May Queen at Ryhall School in 1956 by Sheila Cook.

Meeting the Folks

There were various feast days and each village had one. Mrs Hudson's sister lived at Bisbrook and we used to go to their feast. There were always lots of soft fruits which I loved. There were stalls with lots of food

and home-made beer. Gretton Silver band used to go to nearly all these feast days. The big house would open its grounds and there was bowling for the pig; I used to do well at this and I won several pigs! I used to do well with 'Kill the Rat', when a 'rat' was let down a length of pipe and you had to bash it when it came out. I always used to think things out and there used to be a click as the rat passed a certain point. I used to time that click so I knew when the rat was coming out of the end of the pipe and I hit it every time.

We used to go round people's houses and try home made wine, which was served in pancheons and it was scooped into glasses. It was a chance for relatives to meet up, starting with breakfast and having other meals with different people throughout the day.

Alan Fox

Darts and Skittles

On Feast day the Greetham band used to come to Stretton to play. It always used to rain but that didn't matter. Georgie White's coconut shies and roundabouts used to come from South Witham. and we had darts and skittles. This all happened in a field. We used to bowl for the pig and when I was a bit older I used to roll a beer barrel around.

George Goodwin

A Big Day

Feast Day in Whissendine used to be the first Sunday after 13 July. It was a big day in the village. There were donkey rides and the fair used to come with the roundabouts. The Feast Day used to be held at the Banks but recently it has been in different fields. Where the school is now

was a field and it was held there. It was fun. There were coconut shies and a shooting gallery.

Monica Leclere

Roundabouts and Games

There was always a big Feast Day in Ketton. That took place in the village where the garage is now. There were roundabouts and games for the children. They used to cook a ham for people to eat. There used to be a pub on that site. There were pubs everywhere and at one time there were thirteen.

Georgina Andrews

Putting Up the Flag

Wing always played Ridlington at Cricket on Feast day and then *vice versa* when it was Ridlington's Feast Day. I can't remember much else about it but I know we used to put the flag up.

Raymond Birch

Always a Feast

Wing Feast was always the first Sunday after the 29 June. I think it was stopped at the outbreak of war.

Gladys Birch

Stamford Town Band playing in the Cottage gardens at Ketton Feast, c. 1950.

The Band Played

Ketton Feast was during the first or second week in August. There was a fete one weekend and a band concert the next. The fete took place in the vicarage gardens or Ketton House gardens. I think it has been in Geeston House as well. Stamford Town Band played on one of the Sundays. My father, Alf, played the cornet with them.

Geoff Wright

Roundabouts

In October the roundabouts used to come into the fields next to the Millstone in Ryhall. The Empingham Feast was always the last week of June, and Ryhall was towards the end of October. It used to last the week although there weren't a lot of pennies to spend on the rides. The chapels had a big do. I remember in Empingham they put a platform in the chapel and we did action songs and recitations. Near May Day, Mrs Pugh from the Hall at Ryhall would invite the children to have tea there.

May Wright

All Very Exciting

Ridlington had a feast day but I can't remember very much happening. What I do remember was August Bank Holiday Monday and the County Show at

Oakham. The show was held on what is now Cricket Lawns. It is all built on now. There was a flower show and my grandfather, being a great gardener, liked to enter his flowers. I remember him showing roses. My mother would do a floral basket to enter. We would start out from Ridlington at about half past six in the morning because you had to have your entries into the show very early for the judging. There was always a cricket match, which bored me stiff but there was a band and a concert party. It was all very exciting. On the Thursday before the Bank Holiday, there was a show for the animals. My grandfather received several long service awards from Mr Wortley, the farmer he worked for, and these were presented at the Thursday show.

Elsie Rose

All Sorts of Exhibitions

On August Bank Holiday, which was at the beginning of August then, there was the County Show at Oakham. There were all sorts of exhibitions and trade stalls, and there was a ring for demonstrations for horses and motorcycles. There were displays by the fire brigade. These went on for the whole day. It was a family day.

Maurice Wade

The Rutland Show

Rutland Agricultural Show was always held on the first Monday in August which was the original August Bank Holiday. It was held on the Barleythorpe Road and

Alf Wright played in Stamford Town Band. He is pictured (around 1947) showing one of his four sons how to play the cornet.

became known as Oakham Show. The day changed to the Sunday and then it was brought from Oakham to Burley. When it came to Burley we always started it off with a fete in the village. Mrs Hoare at the vicarage used to have a horse called Lovesong and she used to give rides and we had cake stalls and white elephant stalls. It was to raise money for cancer.

Ray Hill

A Nice Day Out

Oakham Show was always something to look forward to. It was marvellous and it was always a nice day out.

Christine Baum

A Typical Country Show

They held the Oakham Show on the Barleythorpe Road. It was a typical country show and there was mainly livestock. The bulls were always impressive. When it wasn't a showground it was Oakham's rugby ground.

Eddie Butcher

The Show

The Women's Institute stall was always well represented at the Oakham Show. My friend in the village did the fruitcake and the jam and I made the Victoria sponge and the bottled fruit.

May Wright

Gymkhana

We used to take out ponies from Ayston to Oakham for the gymkhana events at Oakham Show. It was about six miles but there was no traffic in those days. We did sack races and things like that. We would have to ride so far and then jump off and get in a sack and jump to the finishing line.

Di Scott

Blands Buses

August Saturday was the agricultural fair on the Barleythorpe Road and the Rutland Horticultural Society people used to have a big tent there. My grandfather was on the committee and later on father was secretary. They had a very big tent there with all the competition entries. My uncles at Hambleton used to bring the shire horses down to the show. My uncle John Parker used to show them for Mr Wild who was a big farmer.

Blands used to run buses to Skegness. They ran a bus there every Sunday. Some people would go one Sunday and come back the next.

Eileen Snow

Diana Scott (nee Robinson) and her sister Clare on their ponies, Dandy and Nippy at Oakham Show in 1937.

Awayday

When we went away we used to go to Skegness for a day out or maybe Hunstanton.

Christine Baum

Sunday School Outing

Once a year there was the Sunday School outing and you either went to the seaside or to Wicksteed Park at Kettering.

Maurice Wade

Trips to the Seaside

Ketton Young Wives Group used to organize trips to the seaside. We went to Cleethorpes, Mablethorpe, Skegness or Hunstanton. I remember one lad wandering off at Cleethorpes, we think, and there was a big police search for him. He had wandered up the beach towards Grimsby. That held up our return.

Geoff Wright

New Hat

We always had to wear a hat to church and Sunday school. I always had a new hat for

Whit Sunday, not for Easter. I had a new dress at Easter. It was rolled up and put in a big cardboard Easter egg.

We always went to the Feasts and I especially liked the Braunston and Langham Feasts.

Eileen Snow

Patterns

On May Day there used to be a maypole at the school and we used to dance around it, holding a ribbon and making patterns at the top of the pole.

Monica Leclere

Queen of the May

I was a May Queen in Preston in the early 1920s. All the children used to vote for the May Queen and I remember the year before me another child was chosen and I was very cross it wasn't me! But I was chosen the next year. We paraded round the village. We used to go round collecting flowers from anyone with a garden and then the boys would decorate two wooden hoops, one put one way and one the other. If one of the girls had a nice doll it was fastened inside the May garland. Then a pole was pushed through it and two boys would carry it on their shoulders.

Gladys Birch

Garland of Hoops

May Day was always an important day when I was at Preston school. A garland was made from a couple of hoops, one inside the other, and the children would collect spring flowers which were wrapped around the hoops by some of the older people in the village. When it was made, the boys would carry it and the girls followed in white dresses, singing songs and doing some country dancing. They would collect money and at the end everyone would have tea.

Elsie Rose

A Big Event

May Day was a big event in Barrowden. I would go round the village with the school singing and some of the children would carry a garland of flowers.

Maurice Wade

Singing Songs

On May Day we used to go round singing the May songs. They used to pick a May Queen out and we'd parade around the village and the toffs would give you money. In the afternoon there was a tea. It was all to do with the church then. At Christmas we always had a school concert.

Raymond Birch

May Day in Barrowden outside the village school. Alan Fox's daughter Angela (now Smith) is fourth from the right on the front row.

Dancing

We used to have May Day celebrations in the school yard at Ketton and the May Queen was crowned there. The schoolchildren danced round the maypole.

Geoff Wright

Pinning the Tail on the Donkey

I was at home with my parents for a year and, of course, I was involved in the life of the parish. There was the brass to be cleaned for a start! I used to organize dances in the village hall and I might join my mother's working parties that made things for the fêtes. All sorts of things happened at the fêtes. There was bowling for the pig, a tombola, a Chinese Laundry when you had small hoops to throw over pegs on a line, and Pinning the Tail on the Donkey. There was usually a board with different numbered holes in it and people had to try and throw bean bags through these holes. The person with the highest score was the winner. One of the most popular events was the dog show and there was always a prize for the dog that looked most like its owner! And of course, we always had a good cake stall. Victoria

Hambleton Summer Fete in 1959 with Sarah Codrington of Preston Hall, the Reverend Hugh Westland and Major Hoare of Hambleton Hall.

sponges went very well and so did scones. We used to run competitions for guessing the weight of a fruitcake too.

Dorothy Westland

Shedding Needles

We used to make Christmas cakes and puddings at the end of October. I would ice the cakes in December. We used to bring the tree in about a fortnight before Christmas but I didn't like it because it shed all its needles so it went out on Boxing Day! Norway used to give Oakham a tree every year and that stood in the market place. Underneath, there were bins so that people could give for charity. When you came out of a shop, you were expected to take something out of your basket and put it in the charity bin.

Anne Spencer

A Big Table of Food

Life was so much more exciting. At Christmas we had one major present but the rest were small like a tin of toffees, an orange and an apple in a stocking. We decorated the Christmas tree on Christmas Eve. We had turkey and mother always cooked a big gammon and made trifles, jellies and blancmanges. She made all her own mince pies. There was always a big table of food at Christmas.

Christine Baum

Goose

We brought our Christmas tree into the house on Christmas Eve. We always had goose for lunch on Christmas Day. In November we had killed a pig and another at the end of January, so we had our own hams. The bacon used to hang in the kitchen to dry and you cut a piece off it and sliced it for frying.

John Tabrum

A Tree and Father Christmas

My dad used to work for the Kimbles at Barleythorpe Hall. We used to go there every Christmas. There was a lovely, big Christmas tree and someone used to dress up as Father Christmas. After tea we used

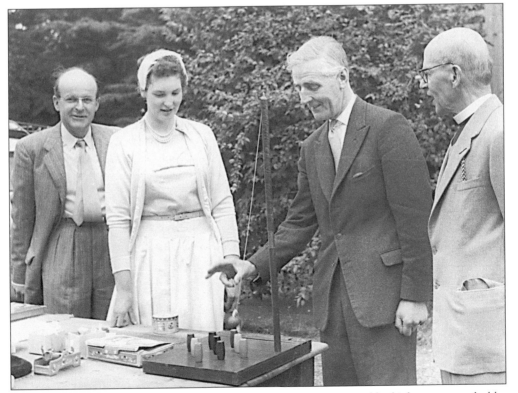

In the gardens of Hambleton Hall, the owner Major Hoare tries out a table skittles game watched by the Reverend Hugh Westland and other visitors.

to sit round the Christmas tree and Mrs Kimble would call out our names and we would go up and get a present.

Eunice Hill

A Wriggly Thing

Lady Codrington was at the Hall in Preston and we always had a Christmas party every year in the school. Every child had a present. First there was the Christmas tea. The top part of the school would be curtained off with the Christmas tree behind it and when you'd had your tea, they would draw the curtains back. You would go up and curtsey to Lady Codrington and she would give you your present. One year I had a wriggly thing which you wound up and it ran along the floor. Another year I had a doll. They were always nice presents. There was always about two weeks at Christmas when you went to parties at your friends and neighbours.

Gladys Birch

The Circus

The circus used to come to Oakham and the big top was in a field at the bottom of Parkfield Road. There were lions and tigers and the elephants used to come by train and walk up from the station advertising the circus.

Eunice Hill

London Sunday

I used to take Kitty to the Picture House in Stamford and we used to go dancing in the Assembly Rooms to the music of Eddie Edinburgh. We went to Hawley's the cycle shop, and we always went to the Mid-Lent fair. The fair went from Stamford to Grantham on what we used to call London Sunday. They used to stop at the Ram Jam garage and whatever they bought, such as petrol or oil, they used to pay for in bags of coppers.

George Goodwin

A New Dress

You always had a new dress at Easter and you always had new sandals. The joke was that once Easter arrived, you didn't have to wear a liberty bodice any more! They had rubber buttons. You'd wear a cardigan with your new dress. When you were very small you wore a straw bonnet. We had very pretty dresses and some had smocking on the front. We only had one egg for Easter and we always had a turkey. There was Christmas, Easter, Whitsuntide and August Bank Holiday and that was all.

Christine Baum

Red, White and Blue

The fair at Oakham was held in Cutts Close which is now the park. The dodgems was the most exciting. I only came to Stamford fair once when I lived in Oakham. To come to Stamford from Oakham was like going to London years ago! I don't ever remember coming to Stamford when I was young. We might go to Leicester on the old steam train. For the Coronation in 1953 we took a train from Oakham to London for the day. I wore a red, white and blue candy-striped dress, a white cardigan and blue and white sandals. It was a big outing to go on a steam train. You slid the doors of the carriage back and there were seats for five each side in each compartment. There was a corridor connecting the compartments and the guard used to come along and look at your tickets.

Christine Baum

Celebrating

In Coronation year, 1953, there were various floats going round the village. On one, somebody had made a great big boot, out of wire and paper mache, on the theme, There was An Old Woman Who Lived in a Shoe, and I was one of the children. Then we all went back to Ketton Club for a party.

Geoff Wright

Motorbike and Sidecar

Cars were uncommon and very few people could afford them. My father bought a motorbike and sidecar in about 1923. He was born in Surrey and for a holiday we went from Oakham to Charwood in Surrey. My mother sat in the sidecar, I sat on her knee and my sister sat on the pillion. We travelled straight through London and my father always wore his cap on backwards or it blew off.

Eddie Butcher

Visiting the Base

We once had a school outing to Spanhoe aerodrome near Harringworth where the Americans were. That was at the end of the war. The American soldiers came and collected us in their great big wagons and took us to the base. They gave us some gum and showed us the aeroplanes and we were allowed to clamber into them and look around. They also showed us their quarters where they were living. I was only about six at the time.

Maurice Wade

Impressive

When the fair came to Oakham it was held on the Lime Kilns which was the cricket field. I remember going on the dragons and it was always impressive with the big steam engines that drove the dynamos. You had the smell of the engines and the fire and the oil lamps that were used. There was quite an atmosphere. The Lime Kilns were owned by Charles Matkin who was a printer and had a shop in the town. It was on the corner of the square in the High Street. Opposite was the Crown which was *the* pub in those days. At one time there was about fifty pubs. The Crown was a coaching house and there was a large yard in the back and it led into South Street.

Eddie Butcher

CHAPTER 7
Village Life

Frank Ellis, 1929.

Idyllic

You didn't realise it at the time but life went on in an idyllic manner in the village. Nothing much really changed. Barrowden was a self-contained village with four pubs that I remember. There was the Exeter Arms, the Crown, the Windmill and the Swan. There was also the Wheel but that had gone before my time. My grandfather bought the Swan as a house. In the 1930s Barrowden had two bakers, a butcher, a blacksmith, two cobblers, four village shops and its own school. The International Stores traveller used to come round early in the week to pick up your order and the van would deliver it to you.

Some time in the 1920s my father, Frank Ellis, met my mother who was nursemaid to the children of Captain Stanley at Tixover Grange when he worked there. He was dismissed when he was caught courting her in the woods!

Robin Ellis

Winifred Wade in the 1940s, inside the village shop which she opened in Rose Villa, Barrowden in 1935.

Clem Robinson with his father-in-law, Dick Clarke walking in the gardens of Ayston Hall.

Farming Ever Since

I was born in Uppingham in North Street but we moved to Ayston when I was two years old. There were two farms belonging to the Fludges and Finches estate, and Vere Finch had the estate in those days. The two farms were let and my grandfather took one on but he died soon after and my father took it on. Then he was offered Home Farm which was the next door farm so we moved there and have been farming it ever since.

Di Scott

General Stores

My mother and father started a shop in Barrowden in 1935. My father was in the saddlery business, which had been in our family since 1736. They were saddlers and harvest makers. When the binders came in for cutting the corn, they mended the canvas that came round the rollers that were used to make the corn ready for the stooks. I can remember helping to mend these canvasses which had wooden laths on them. That business was dying because gradually tractors and combine harvesters came along. It was most likely mother's idea to get the shop going. They made their house, which at the time was called Rose Villa, into a shop. They sold just about everything; groceries, sweets, ice creams. I used to bag up lard and sugar. The wholesalers sent us a half hundred weight sack of sugar and I had to weigh it out into thick blue bags. I had to learn the special way of fastening the top so that the sugar didn't come out! In 1944 they started a post office in the shop and that

Winnie and Eddie Wade outside their shop in Barrowden, 1936.

brought in more income.

My father still worked in the saddlery business until 1956. He delivered the letters in Wakeley and Mrs Cranfield delivered the letters in Barrowden. The postmen from Oakham brought the mail to the village very early in the morning and they were sorted in the saddlers' workshop at Barrowden. Then, after his delivery, my father went on to do his work at the saddlery.

There was another shop in Chapel Lane. This was run by a family called Stapleton and then a Mr Goodwin bought it and he was followed by a family called Cliff.

Every fortnight or so, a traveller, a commercial traveller I suppose, would come and take the order of things my mother needed for the shop and then they would be delivered. In later years we also sold bread which mother bought from a firm in Peterborough called Fowlers. She bought wrapped, sliced bread and that didn't go down too well with the local baker. In 1948 she bought a fridge and we sold ice creams. They were wrapped oblong pieces and you'd have to unwrap them and put them between two wafers. She also had blocks of ice cream that she used to cut up and then we sold ice lollies.

At first there was just the one room in the middle and then there was the lounge at the back where we had the organ and we used that on a Sunday. Not so long after the war, mother opened that back room up for selling toys.

Maurice Wade

The Worst Job

I used to work on Pridmore's farm at Luffenham with Charlie Horton and Dan

Beasley when I was ten. When it came to thrashing time, the thrashing tackle used to be hired either from Bill Storey's at Barrowden or the Ellam's at Ashwell. The first year you did it you got the worst job. That was in the porthole where all the rubbish used to come in and you had to keep it clear. It would fall all over you, all over your face and it would get in your clothes. Then from that you might go on to cutting the bands to put the sheaves in and after that you might go up the straw stack with the jack.

Alan Fox

Gleaning

When I was a boy, my sister, me and my mother used to go from Empingham to Tickencote to go gleaning. The Barwells next door went too. My father used to have the gleaning thrashed. Sometimes he used to put it in the copper to make some beer, but mostly it was for the pig. We lived at that time in Mill Lane and we always had a pig each year. We used to go to Mr Hudson's and to Mr Reeve's and to Crossroads farm. When we went gleaning we used to have to ask permission from the farmer to go in the fields. We used to fill up sacks and we piled them in the wash house. I took the last four bags of corn to be ground at the mill here in Empingham.

Arthur Branson

Out All Day

There used to be an old girl who lived next door to us here, Mrs Bagley her name was. She

The wedding of Dorothy Stafford and Alfred Wright at Ketton in 1945. From left to right, Ken Fountain, the bride and groom, Gladys Stafford, and the bride's father, Percival Stafford.

used to be out all day gleaning. You'd see her go by at nine o'clock, after the farmers had raked it in, and you'd see her come back at twelve o'clock with her apron on top of her head. She took scissors with her and brought back just the heads. She wouldn't bring the straw. Then she went back.

Raymond Birch

went gleaning. The farmer always left a sheaf in the field to tell us we could go and glean. It was mostly mothers and children who gleaned. We picked up all the fallen ears, and there were quite a lot in those days. We collected handfuls and mother put them in a bigger bag and we'd use them to feed the hens.

Robin Ellis

A Sheaf Left in the Field

After the harvest was cut, and the sheaves were taken away and the rake went through to collect up whatever fallings there were, we

Starting Early

My father had a car but he hated driving. He had a licence even though in those days you didn't have to pass a test. He worked all the time – until about nine o'clock in the evening. He used to start early in the morning and he even worked on a Saturday. At night he used to have his pork pie for supper – every night. He'd get the old mustard out and the teapot going. He was a Baptist so he never worked on a Sunday.

Maurice Wade

Firewatchers

I was born, baptised, confirmed and, in 1936, married in Empingham. In those days everybody made their own amusements in the village because there was no television. Children went out to play. When we married we moved to the square in Ryhall and after eighteen months we took this house on the Turnpike Road. We could have had a house in Empingham but Granny Wright thought it would be too far for Joe to bike the five and a half miles to work every day. He was working then at Martins in Stamford. Since I first moved here Ryhall has almost doubled in size. There were no houses beyond the vicarage and the village hall.

During the war Joe and I were firewatchers. With being in the St John's Ambulance Brigade – I was a nurse for eight years and Joe was a member for forty something years – we were on call to go and render first aid if anything happened. We cycled to Stamford for meetings. Monday nights were the nurses' evening. In the summer we had the big inspection for the Lincoln area and he had to go to places like Grantham, Spalding and Sleaford.

There was a pub on the corner of Turnpike Road in Ryhall called The Tally Ho and the men who used to train for the ARP on Sunday mornings, they used to use that. Cards and dominoes were played there. Joe and I were both big crib (cribbage) players and we won a lot of cups and trays. Joe played for the Plough at Casterton and I played for the Millstone in Ryhall. There were quite a few pubs but only the two are left now. When we lived in the square there was the Green Dragon and Joe could pop across there in his slippers! That's what he liked! The Five Bells was in the square and there was once one next to the chapel.

May Wright

Shoeing Horses

The blacksmith's shop in Whissendine has gone now and there's a new house in its place. It was just above the church and opposite the old vicarage. I remember my father shoeing horses and repairing the rims on the wagon wheels. They made candle sticks for Heal's of London.

I met my husband at one of our village dances in Whissendine. He was in the air force at Cottesmore.

Everybody went to church or chapel on a Sunday. There were two chapels, Methodist and Wesleyan. We used to have to go to Sunday School, morning and afternoon.

Monica Leclere

Good Times

Mrs Wright, the vicar's wife, asked me if I would help her form a Women's Institute in

Three Generations. Henry James Wade with his son, Eddie who is holding Maurice.

Joe Wright in his St John's Ambulance uniform with his wife, May, on a day out in Skegness.

Ryhall with two other people. We had about twenty members to start with and we met at the village hall. In those days it was called the Working Men's Club and it was a tin hut. The working men built it in their spare time. There was a big old iron stove in the middle which never threw out much heat. We had some good times there. Mrs Wright was the first president.

May Wright

Timing the Sermon

On Sundays we would walk to the eleven o'clock service at Stretton church and in the afternoon we went back to Sunday School. Then, in the evening, we would walk back with my parents for the six o'clock service. If the sermon went on too long, Major Hesketh, who sat at the front, would take his watch out and put it where the parson could see it and know he should stop.

George Goodwin

The Sunday Roast

There was a general store which had two windows next to the pub in Whissendine. There were three butchers, another shop on the Stapleford Road and four bakers. Some people put their Sunday roast in Green's baker's oven while they went to church. Green's bakery was next door to the Three Horseshoes. There was a shoemaker, too.

In the evenings the men used to go to the pub for a drink and there used to be whist drives and concerts. My dad used to go and sing at the concerts in the village hall. They sang things like 'My Grandfather's Clock'. The women would knit or go to the Mothers' Union or the Women's Institute.

Monica Leclere

Walks on Sunday

My mother was secretary of the Baptist chapel in Barrowden and she arranged for preachers to come from other Baptist chapels around. Sometimes the Methodist preachers would come and occasionally some from the Pentecostal church. There was only one service on a Sunday starting at six at night and lasting about an hour. Mother played the organ and I sat behind it and pumped it! The preachers would often come to tea first because of transport problems. If they came from Morcott they would cycle, or they might come by bus or train from Peterborough or Oakham. Then we'd have to drive them from Luffenham station.

We'd often go for walks on a Sunday as a family. I had a car numbering craze and on a Sunday evening my father and I would walk up to the Leicester road, now the A47, and I would sit down and take car numbers for a while. He had a job to get me away!

Maurice Wade

Half Day Off

I was at the Red House for four or five years and then I married the blacksmith's son, William but he was always known as Bill. I met him at one of the dances in the village.

Joe Wright is recognised as a blood donor. Presenting him with a bronze medal is Captain Armstrong of the St John's Ambulance Brigade.

He used to come up to the Red House to do something and I used to see him then and I used to go out with him on my half day. We didn't go anywhere special, we just went for a walk. That's what everybody did. If we went to dances we used to go to Oakham; we always wore long dresses. I remember him and his dad making two horseshoes for Oakham Castle. One was for a viscount, I can't remember who, but the other one was for the old Duke of Gloucester. I can also remember Bill's dad making my iron gate. He put Ty Newydd on it because I am Welsh and that means 'new house'. I came to live in this house now since 1937. My husband had it built.

Lucy Wiggington

Bottling Fruit

We used to do bottling and jamming in the war and we used to pickle eggs in isinglass and put them in an earthenware pot. Beans would be preserved in salt and fruit was bottled in Kilner jars.

Monica Leclere

Bell-ringing

I learned to be a bell-ringer at Empingham church. Grace Hall's father, Charlie Wilson, used to ring the first bell. It was hard to get him up the stairs sometimes – he'd had too much beer. But he never made a mistake. He got to know the rhythm of Grandsire Doubles and he knew when to change. There were six of us including Cyril Lambert, Walter Maddison, Jim Brown and Austin Bland. Sometimes Joe Rudkin would come along. I was the youngest at fifteen. We rang every week. Grandsire Doubles had 325 changes. Doctor Seymour stopped me ringing, and stopped me smoking when I was seventy.

Arthur Branson

Twice a Week

There were no buses in those days so we used to walk. I can remember walking to Oakham, which was a good five miles away, with my mother when I was about five or six years old. My mother did her shopping in Uppingham which was only two or three miles away and carried the shopping home. She would go to Uppingham once or twice a week. Having hens, she had one or two customers in the town who bought the eggs. Occasionally they wanted the poultry, which she would dress.

Elsie Rose

Mary Cunnington and Joe Wright were married in 1936 at Empingham. The photograph was taken outside the Cunnington's house in Empingham and shows Grahamme Sorfleet of Stamford as a pageboy wearing a velvet suit, and bridesmaids Florrie (right) who is May's sister, and Edie, Joe's sister. Both came to May and Joe's Golden Wedding celebrations.

Paraffin

Electricity wasn't in all the houses in Barrowden and we sold paraffin which was used to light the lamps. Most people used coal and wood for their fires but would heat a greenhouse with a paraffin heater. I know some people didn't have electricity until the 1960s. And there was no gas.

There were three other pubs in Barrowden apart from the Exeter Arms. Swan House used to be the Swan pub, the Crown was to the north and the Windmill was on the east side.

Maurice Wade

The Choral Society

Up the hill there was Mrs Tarlton who lived at The Rosary. Her gardener used to live next door to us. They would open their grounds once a year. They had a daughter who was a very good soprano and when we had the choral society she used to sing with us. The Reverend Wright, who was the music master at the grammar school in Stamford, lived in The Firs and he used to be in charge of the society. We did ever so well. I've still got a copy of the Hallelujah chorus. We were always short of male singers.

May Wright

Some of the family and friends of Lucy Parker and Edward Pawlett following their wedding at Upper Hambleton in 1913.

Christopher Rowell outside The Lodge in Ridlington with one of his cows.

Making Stilton Cheese

When I was fourteen I went to live with an aunt and uncle who had a farm a few miles out of the village and I was with them for five years. I used to help about the house and the farm. We used to make Stilton cheese in a big vat.

Monica Leclere

Home delivery

When I was eight or nine, the International Stores which was in the main street of Uppingham, started sending round a traveller. He would visit us in Ridlington on a Tuesday and take the order. He would come with a case, on a bicycle, and write the order in a little book. On the Wednesday or the Thursday the order was delivered. We paid when it was delivered or my mother paid in the shop when she was next in town.

Elsie Rose

Biking

We used to ride to Edith Weston, Barrowden, Morcott, and Lyndon to the dances. The Four Ace Band, Marmie Elliott's band, from Manton. Claude Spencer played the piano and 'Judy' Ward played the drums.

Gladys Birch

Lead Singer

We were in the church choir at Burley and there was a choir practice on a Thursday

May Wright (formerly Cunnington) in her St John's Ambulance uniform during the 1940s.

Grace and John Hall cut their wedding cake at the reception following their wedding in July 1941.

night. Mrs Thornton from Oakham played the organ and she took the choir practice. Miss Lane was the main singer. She sang very loudly and if she didn't go to church we missed her because there was nobody else to lead us! When the vicar stopped his preaching everybody was waiting for Miss Lane to start the singing. We had whist drives and social evenings in the village hall and these were to raise money for the church. There was an annual fete and that was also to raise money for the church. Sometimes that was held in the vicarage garden and sometimes at Burley-on-the-Hill, the big house. Mr Finch used to let us use the gardens. There was a special passage from the house to the church so the family didn't have to go outside.

I can remember people skating on the flooded fields at Burley-on-the-Hill. Burley Fishponds is to the east of the causeway and the flooded fields are to the west. On the flooded fields they grew willows and the reeds used for thatching. My friend's mother can remember carrying the reeds up. Her husband was a farmer at Egleton. He used to cut the reeds with a scythe and she used to bundle them up and carry them off. There used to be boards for people to walk on.

Ray Hill

Water from the Well

When the garage was first built they also built a windmill in the field and that pumped water down to the garage. Eventually, the water was laid on to the cottages owned by Major Hesketh in the village. In the old days there was only an old well and we used to wind the buckets up. There were two buckets and it was

seventy-five turns to let one bucket down and the other one up. When you got to the top you gave it half a turn and that lifted the side up and the water came out. But if, when it went down, a stone or something got between the sides and the bottom, when you wound it up again, it was empty! When they put the windmill in, they put a tap where the well is. It was outside our bungalow and other people used to come and fill their buckets. In the winter, if the tap got frozen, Kitty had to thaw it and then go running to everyone to tell them it was thawed if they wanted water.

George Goodwin

Wartime

During the war we had a regiment down the avenue, a hospital at Burley-on-the-Hill, Ashwell camp, and there always used to be some soldiers camping on the village green.

Ray Hill

Bomber Base

The aerodrome at the top of the village was a bomber base and it is an army barracks now. The air force were here until a year ago.

Elsie Rose

Home Guard

I was in 'Dad's Army'! I didn't have to join up in the war because I worked on the land,

The wedding of Raymond Birch and Gladys Wing in October 1938. From left to right: Nora Rate, Bob Birch, Raymond and Gladys, George Wing, Dorothy Birch.

I was in the Home Guard. There was me, Joe Green and his father, Bill Green, Harry Chilcock, Herbert Naylor and loads more. We were with one platoon and we joined up with Morcott. There was Morcott, Wing, Glaiston and Seaton. Our Lieutenant was a schoolmaster from Uppingham. I remember we had to go on dawn patrol; in the summer time that was usually three o'clock in the morning. We had an old hen hut up at the Grange and that was our base. There used to be two of us each time, taking it in turns on a rota. We had to get dressed up with our rifles and it was just for an hour at daybreak. They said that was the time the enemy was likely to come over but we never saw

anything. When they bombed Coventry the sky was really lit up and red and you could see it clearly from here.

Raymond Birch

Double Summer Time

During the war there was double summer time and the clocks used to be moved two hours back or forwards instead of one. I remember playing cricket on the village green at eleven o'clock at night when it was still light. Mother used to have to come and

Aerial view of Eglton church.

Ketton people outside The Cottage following Dorothy Burrough's wedding in 1906. Photograph by Pleasance Burroughs.

fetch me.

When the war was on we had to put shutters up at night and make sure no light escaped from the doors and windows. My father, Thomas Edward Henry Wade, was born in 1900 and he did nine months in the Durham Light Infantry in the first war but he wasn't called up in the second war.

Maurice Wade

Fifty Years On

We had a youth club at Burley and the boys used to come up here from Oakham. One day one said, 'you ought to ask that Eunice Clarke if she wants to go pictures'. I said, 'd'you think she would?', and he said 'yes, give us your photo and I'll take it to show her'. He took this photo down to Oakham and Cora where Eunice worked and said Ray wants to know if you'll go pictures with him. She looked at the photo and said, 'oh no, not that old boy from Burley! Oh no, I don't like him!' But I must have made a bit of an impression because eventually I persuaded her to go pictures. And that's how we started. We've known each other fifty years. We went out with each other for three years, then we got engaged and three years later we got married.

Ray Hill

Walnut Trees

Stretton was noted for its walnut trees. It was surrounded by these trees and people used to bike from the nearby villages to pick walnuts up from the ground.

George Goodwin

Local Shops

In Ketton we used to have a post office, barber's shop, a general store and grocer's, Hallam's shop in Aldgate, and two blacksmiths – one on Stocks Hill and one at the bottom of Bull Lane.

Geoff Wright

Bag of Chips

The fish and chip van always came around on a Wednesday. A chap called Simms from Wing brought it. It came in the evening and I used to listen for it when I was doing my homework. Usually I just had a bag of chips.

Maurice Wade

Damson Trees

We lived in a bungalow opposite the Ram Jam in Stretton. There were two damson trees in the garden and they didn't have much fruit. The old farmer came over one day and he said to me, 'Have you thrashed them?' I said no so he took the clothes prop and he lambasted these trees. The next year we got baths full of damsons so ever after that I used to thrash them!

George Goodwin

The Home Guard on parade in Uppingham during the Second World War.

Village Cricket

I played for the Hambleton cricket team in the 1930s. We had a very peculiar pitch. It was used by cattle as grazing land. The square itself was surrounded by posts with barbed wire to keep the cattle off. Before we started a game we had to lift the posts out of the way. The vicar played for the team. He had a little Ford 8 and unless he played we couldn't have a match because he had to drive three of us to the different grounds. The chap who worked at the post office in Hambleton was called Billy Bushell and he was a leading member of the team. Farmers from Nether Hambleton called Phil and Harry Wakeley also played for us.

Eddie Butcher

Baby Geoff Wright in his pram on the Luffenham Road out of Ketton. In those days prams were heavier and harder to manoeuvre.

An Old BSA

The first bike I had was an old BSA. My sister used to work at Ashwell and if we were going to a dance I would pick her up and then pick Kitty up. I used to sit at the front, Kitty on the seat and my sister on the carrier at the back.

George Goodwin

A Terrible Winter

I can remember my mum talking about the terrible winter of 1916. We had a pump in the paddock across the road where we lived at Preston, and she said you could have walked over the top of the pump and not known it was there because of the hard packed snow.

Gladys Birch

Sledges

When there was really bad weather they used to push the milk round on sledges. My auntie was Betty Tebbutt and she lived in the Lanes.

Georgina Andrews

The Sixth Tree

My mum was born at The Olive Branch in Clipsham in 1875. Her name was Annie Merry. Her parents were Billy and, I think, Sarah Merry and they ran the pub. My dad was born at the Fox and Hounds at Castle Bytham. My sister May remembers standing in the window waiting for the horse and cart to come along and take them to Braunston Lodge where we lived before I was born.

If you look at the trees leading to Clipsham Hall, the sixth tree on the right hand side was cut in memory of Billy Merry. It has a horse on it because he used to ride with the Cottesmore Hounds. I can remember him riding into the yard at Preston, having ridden all the way from Clipsham. All the Merry family are buried at Clipsham churchyard.

Georgina Andrews

Market Day

Every Friday we would go on the bus to Stamford for the market.

Gladys Birch

By Bus or Train

We rarely went to Oakham or Uppingham from Barrowden. The United Counties bus route ran between Uppingham and

John Parker (left) with Lucy Parker (seated on the grass centre right) who looked after Major Fogg's young daughter.

The Parker's house in Middle Hambleton. Arthur Parker lived there until Rutland Water was built. On the lawn was a well which they used for water.

Stamford and that came through Barrowden. Mrs Dixie told us in school that they had undercut a man called Storey from Tinwell who had a little bus service which he ran to Barrowden in the 1930s and he was forced out of business. We had Wakeley Station which was just over the river south of the village, and we used to get a train to Peterborough from there. Wakeley is about half a mile from Barrowden.

Robin Ellis

Collecting

On Saturdays we went round the village collecting salvage which was whatever the government decreed could be recycled at that time. So we collected paper, cardboard, wood, and rubber. There was a shed in the middle of the field by the Exeter Arms – which is now a car park – and all the salvage was taken there. A lorry came round every so often and took it away. We were also sent out during the summer to pick the hedgerows clean of hips and haws. We had to collect nettles by the sackful. They were taken up to the school which was the collecting point. What happened to them after that I've no idea. We were paid a penny for so much collected.

We used to go up to the woods collecting firewood, 'sticking' we called it. We used to go to the A47 and Life Hill where there were two woods at the top. Every September the pastures between Barrowden and the

A47 were then rough grazing land and full of blackberry bushes. If it was a fine afternoon you were sent up blackberry picking.

Robin Ellis

Vicar for Ten Years

My father was Hugh Westland and he was the vicar of Hambleton and Egleton. He was ordained late in life because he worked for the Post Office for forty-two years and retired at sixty. He was ordained in Lincoln Cathedral after many years as a lay reader and, when the living became vacant in 1955, he accepted it.

The vicarage there was a lovely house built on a square plan. There were cellars and attics. From the top attics you could look out across the Vale of Catmos. We had a Rayburn in the kitchen, which was an absolute joy, but it was a huge kitchen and difficult to keep warm. There were stone flags in the hall. Mother used to alternate the rooms that had fires to keep the place aired. My father's study was smaller and that had a fire. Coal, bread, meat and milk were

Three young men from Barrowden way in the 1940s. From left to righ: Lewis Webster, Robin Long, Robin Ellis.

Rosemary Ellis, now Roberts, in front of her father's Ford 8 at The Chestnuts in Barrowden.

The vicarage at Hambleton; at this time Hugh Westland was the Incumbent.

all delivered. The baker was Mr Strickland and he kept a shop in Oakham. We had no heating in the bedrooms at the vicarage. There were shutters at the windows in my bedroom but still in winter the ice used to form on the inside of the glass. I remember my father bringing a paraffin heater up to warm my room sometimes, it was *so cold*. We put apples in the attic to keep them over the winter. There was a big pantry and my mother used to bottle pears during the summer for the winter and she made a lot of jam.

Dorothy Westland

Helping Out

When I was at Casterton school, I used to go and help with the milk bottling at Skinners at Manor Farm in the High Street. They'd milk the cows, tip the milk through a filter and a cooler and then tip the filtered cooled milk into a container that filled them and put a cap on. Then we had to hose all the bottles down. That was in the evening ready for delivery the next morning. We didn't get paid for it, you just went and helped out.

Geoff Wright

The Post Office

There were about a hundred inhabitants of Hambleton and sixty in Egleton. There was no help to be had in the village for the vicarage. There was no transport either except on a Wednesday when there was one bus that came through the village in the

Shire horses owned by Mr Wild, farmer from Upper Hambleton.

During re-decoration of St Edmunds church at Egleton in 1961, a wall painting was discovered depicting the coat of arms of George I.

The Reverend Hugh Westland.

The Reverend Hugh and Mrs Beatrice Westland.

afternoon and took us down to Oakham. I had a bicycle and I would cycle into Oakham until we eventually got a car and I learnt to drive. There was no shop in the village but there was a pub and a post office. It was a very unusual post office because it had a lot of little plants decorating it. It was kept by Aggie Bushell and her husband, Billy and the post office was really in the front room of their cottage.

Dorothy Westland

Ayston. From left to right: Clem Robinson, Diana Robinson, Nellie Robinson, Lizzie Aldred, Lancelot Lowther, John Scott, Clare Robinson, Bob Robinson, James Finch and Frank Freeman, ex-huntsman of the Pytchley Hunt.

CHAPTER 8

Town Talk

From left to right: George Pawlett, Lucy and Edward Pawlett, Doris Pawlett and young 'Pet' Pawlett outside their house in John Street, Oakham.

A Quiet Place

Oakham was a very quiet place while I was growing up. You knew everyone in the town and you always spoke to everyone. The post office used to be right down at the bottom of the High Street where the art shop is. There used to be Bon Marche on the corner and Mr Stephens, the gents outfitter, was next door.

Then there was the bank, the Crown Hotel, and Wellingtons was next to the Crown – that's where Boots is now. Then there was Jackson & Boston's, the ironmongers and Drusilla, which was a ladies' hat shop. Furley's was a wine shop. Mr Hart the grocer was next to Flore's House, then Clarkes the grocers and Mr Wakefield who sold toys. Above Mr Wakefields was a hairdressers. There was

Dick Clarke and Tom Tabrum in Uppingham High Street.

A group of men who belonged to the Red Cross during the war, around 1940 in Oakham. On the front row, second left, is Edward Pawlett and second right is Charles Cave.

another Mr Stephens who was a gent's outfitter and next to him was Freeman, Hardy and Willis and then a garage.

Miss Freeborough had a high-class ladies' clothes shop and I worked for her for a while. I would take all the alterations back to her customers when they were finished. Her husband used to have a jeweller's shop the other side of the street called Smiths. Just before Miss Freeborough's was the fish shop and little Mrs Grimmer had the sweet shop.

Eunice Hill

Youth Club

We used to go to the Tipples which was down Burley Road in Oakham. It was where the old doctor's surgery was and where the opticians is now. There were swings and roundabouts there. There was a youth club we went to which was next to the old Bell pub. That used to stand on the corner where the library is. Then there were the Girl Guides, which used to meet at Burley Road school.

Christine Baum

Cubs

When John and I were courting we use to walk a lot and we had a tandem so we used to ride a lot as well. We ran a cub pack before we were married. We were married by the Reverend Prytherch at Oakham church,

The front of The Falcon Inn, Uppingham at the beginning of the twentieth century. Note the entrance for coaches and horses.

he was the chaplain to the scouts. We lived at the side of the scout headquarters in Northgate Street. Years ago it had been a pub and then it was taken over by the British Legion. When they moved to the High Street the Scouts moved in. The Scouts had the long room upstairs and we had a kitchen and a living room on that floor and then we went up some more stairs to the bedroom.

Eileen Snow

Hair Cut

Uppingham was the place where I had to cycle every other week to get my hair cut. It was a rigid thing and if you didn't get it cut you were in trouble with the housemaster. Robert Duesbury was our housemaster and he was very fair but often we would be sent to the barber in Oakham.

Maurice Wade

Four Slaughterhouses

Dick Cliff was a jeweller in Uppingham and his brother, Cecil was a butcher. There were a lot of butchers in Uppingham and I think there were four slaughterhouses which were attached to the butchers. Perkins sold most things for men and women and they were next door to The Falcon overlooking the market place. Bertie Barnes had a shop on the corner of the market place and he was a gents' outfitters. Mrs Hudson owned a bicycle shop in Orange Street.

Di Scott

A Big Village

When I first lived in Oakham it was a big village. We had some lovely shops, though. I remember there was Hassan's which was an old-style shop that sold everything. and they restored furniture. It was a very big shop that had lots of different parts to it. There were some lovely jewellers in the town too. I used to buy my groceries at a little shop in Dean Street and there was a Co-op on the corner of Dean Street and the High Street, and an International Stores. The shops used to serve you. I used to make a list in a book and they delivered what I wanted. They sent it with a little boy on a bike. Then, when I went to pay the bill the next week, I put in another list of what I needed. You never carried things in those days. The butcher used to come to the door and the baker came. There was a man who came selling greengroceries. You didn't have to go out. Near us there was a post office and two or three other little shops. One sold haberdashery and I remember there was a fruit shop.

Anne Spencer

E. Bird, coal merchant, with his horse and cart in Uppingham.

Ladling the Milk

I remember going round the town with milk in buckets. We had a horse and trap and then later a car with a trailer. We would put the bucket and the churn in the trap and then take the bucket of milk and go around the houses with a ladle. The back door would always be unlocked and a jug would be sitting on the table. You would just pour in the pint of milk or the two pints, whatever they wanted. You never saw anybody! It was quite common in those days to wander in and out of other people's houses.

We did some bottling. Some people liked their milk in jugs and others liked it packaged! We filled bottles by hand. There was a special measure that you dipped in the churn. There was a spout on it that went in the neck of the bottle. Then you put a cardboard lid on it. Then we progressed to using a foil cap, which you put over the top of the bottle and then you had a thing you pushed over it to seal it.

We made cream and butter. My mother did it but my father made it too. Because we sold mainly milk and cream, anything that was left over was made into butter mainly for our own consumption, we didn't sell much butter. To make it we used a big wooden churn – which I think is now across at the school and used as a tombola drum! It was huge, at least two feet long, and there were fixed paddles in it. When we wanted to make only a small quantity, we used a glass jar with an attachment at the top, which had a paddle in it, and you just wound the handle until you got butter. Sometimes it went quickly, sometimes it went slowly.

John Tabrum

The Stirrup Cup

Lord Sefton had a racing stable in Oakham and on a Monday morning a string of racehorses with their grooms came to the front door of the Cross Keys and mother would take out the stirrup cup to them.

Eddie Butcher

A Box with Two Wheels

In the wartime, my brothers were older than me and they were in the forces. Coal was scarce then and it was rationed, my sister and I had to push an old truck, that was like a wooden box with two wheels, down to the coal yard near the station. We had to take it for the groceries too because there wasn't any deliveries.

Eunice Hill

The Cross Keys

I had a little dog and if you came in the back way of the pub from John Street you could go right through it and come out in New Street. I used to chase around with the dog from one side to the other. It was a most peculiar place. The pub consisted of a bar for men only, a sitting room opposite which we would allow friends to use, a ballroom which was always full of people on a Saturday night, and a long bar, or Tap Room with the cellar on the far side of it. Outside the Tap Room was a yard and opposite was the kitchen. Above the kitchen was a permanent ladder and that led to a room

Albert Butcher and Annie his wife (formerly Gatehouse) who ran the Cross Keys in Oakham.

which we hired out to a cobbler. Over the Tap Room was another long open room which we used to let to a butcher. There was a door in the outer wall with a little gantry and he could haul the carcasses up to the room. On the other side of the yard was a double garage going out into John Street and on the left as you went out were three more bedrooms that we used for travellers. They were mostly commercial travellers.

Eddie Butcher

Walking

I can remember the judge and jury used to walk to the Assizes, in wigs and gowns, from the judge's house in the High Street in Oakham.

I used to take my children to the infant's school, which was ever such an old building. Every day I used to collect them and give them some sandwiches and take them for a walk through the fields. They have built Cora's there now.

Anne Spencer

Wearing a Hat

We used to go to the Methodist chapel in Northgate Street. Mr Dennison, who was the butcher used to go. So did Mrs Carter who sang very loudly. If you were talking, she used to get her walking stick and clout you with it! Everyone used to wear hats for chapel in those days.

Eunice Hill

In First Gear

In the square in Oakham there was another pub called The George. It's now called the Whipper Inn. It was a coaching inn and the entrance was blocked up. In that square, on the castle side, was an ironmonger's shop run by a chap called Tommy Perkins. In those days, compared with the present day, some people were a bit unworldly. A lot had never even been to London.

One day somebody was trying to sell Perkins a motorbike. This chap started it up and suggested Perkins sat on it to get the feel. Perkins said he couldn't balance so the chap put it in first gear and gave him a push. He went off and when he got to the end of the square he turned left and then he turned right down Mill Street and all the time he's calling out 'How do I stop it? How do I stop it?' He went all the way round the town in first gear, along South Bank and then back down the High Street.

Eddie Butcher

Entertainment

There was an operatic society in Uppingham and we used to put on Gilbert and Sullivan operettas. The headmaster's wife, Mrs Lloyd, got me interested in taking part. I was in the chorus. John Tabrum's father was interested in theatricals. There was also a youth club and Aunt Dolly and Uncle Tom used to run it. They produced quite a lot of plays. This used to be in the winter when there was not much else on. The Young Farmer's Club was formed in the late 1940s.

Di Scott

On stage in Uppingham. From left to right: Elsie Dickens, Tom Tabrum, -?-, -?-, Kath Dickens, Maurice Baines, Frances Clarke.

Cattle Market

There was a cattle market in Oakham every Friday in South Street.

Christine Baum

Pork Pies

My mother always bought her pork pies from Nelson the butcher who had a shop near the station. As you went up the High Street, you went past the modern cinema on the right, The County. On the right where Dean Street started was the Co-op on the corner. Dulcie Ellingworth ran a little music shop near there and she only sold sheet music. There was a thatched cottage on the right where one of my old teachers from the Church of England school lived. Opposite was the White Lion and then you carried on passed the Congregational church on the left and then you came to a row of four shops. Nelson the Butchers was one of those.

Eddie Butcher

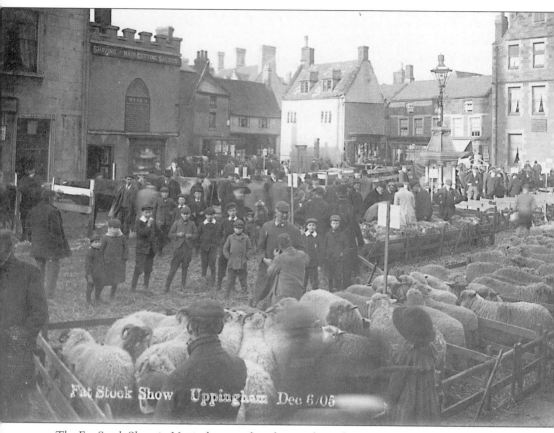

Fat Stock Show   Uppingham   Dec 6/05

The Fat Stock Show in Uppingham market place in the early 1900s.

Twenty-two minutes to Oakham

Oakham was eight miles away and I used to go there on my push-bike to do my courting. It took twenty-two minutes. I met my wife, Eleanor Kate Palmer but she was always known as Kitty, at the Victoria Hall in Oakham. We were married for sixty-three and a half years. I stood in the entrance of the Victoria Hall and these two beautiful girls came in and I knew the one I was going to marry. That was how I met her and it was love at first sight. The Reverend Basil Whealdon from Stretton married us at Oakham church.

When we went to dances at the Victoria Hall we had to take our dancing shoes with us. We would go on Saturday night hops. You were not allowed on the dance floor in ordinary outdoor shoes. If you wanted a drink you had to go downstairs for a cup of tea or a glass of beer. We would do waltzes, quadrilles, The Lancers, St Bernard's Waltz, the Military Two-step, and the Tango. One of most embarrassing moments was when I was dancing with a girl and she twirled round and left me with a hairpiece on my thumb! She grabbed it and tore off!

Kitty and I would go to a lady in Oakham and have a glass of port with her before the dance. She always liked to see we were nicely dressed. Kitty always wore long evening dresses and sometimes, for the bigger dances, I wore black tie. The Servant's Hunt Ball took place once a year in the Victoria Hall. All the hunt servants from around the county came and it was a very popular occasion. There used to be policemen on the doors when it was the Hunt Ball.

George Goodwin

Hoop Skirts

We used to go dancing at the Victoria Hall on Friday nights and it cost five shillings. There was always a good band. I remember the John Anthony Quintet which was run by Tony Gilbert. We did rock 'n roll. I can see mother now starching my net petticoat. Some petticoats had a hoop skirts. You threaded the plastic-covered wire through narrow folds in the skirt, one at the hem and another about eighteen inches above it. We wore circular skirts and waspie belts. There was never any bother at the dances in those days.

Christine Baum

The Cottesmore and the Quorn

The main hunt was the Cottesmore and there were others around such as the Quorn and the Pytchley. Boxing Day was the main meet of the year which was held in the park at Oakham. There would be, perhaps, 200 horses there and everyone went down there to see them.

Eddie Butcher

The Gang Show

Oakham always had a wonderful Gang Show which was held at the Victoria Hall. Charlie Underwood was in it. He had a lot to do with the Scouts.

Christine Baum

Treading the Boards

I was the secretary of Oakham Theatrical Society and one of the men was a steward at Ashwell open prison. He asked me if I would

George William Henry Goodwin and Eleanor Kate Palmer (Kitty) on their wedding day, 27 April 1935.

Dorothy Westland.

consider taking part in a play with some of the men at the prison because they had reached saturation point choosing plays without women in them. So I took part in a play called *The Public Prosecutor*, which was about the French Revolution.

Dorothy Westland

No Lodge Farms

Uppingham is an unusual place because there are no lodge farms. A lodge farm is where you have a farm, on its own, with all the land around it. In Uppingham, all the land was privately owned by a lot of people; everybody owned a field or two, and there were no big estates. Uppingham is unusual in that respect and all the farm yards and farmhouses were actually in the town and the land was outside. There used to be a farmyard in the late 1930s where the Central Garage is now. We had our first tractor about 1955. Before that we used horses. I can remember when we had two blacksmiths in Uppingham. That would be in the late forties or early fifties, and there were two or three ironmongers.

John Tabrum

Market Day

Monday was market day in Oakham and the farmers would bring their cattle up New Street

The Catmose Dance Band Players in the 1920s. From left to right: Raymond Perfect, Fred Rising, Billy Swindale, and Bill Wiggington. The name of the pianist is unknown.

and down to South Street where the market was. Other boys and I used to go up to the level crossing and ask the farmers if they wanted any help. On one or two occasions I helped out which meant standing in the side streets with a stick to make sure the cattle didn't stray off the road. For that I got the princely sum of a shilling.

My father used to buy a full Stilton in the market and that was available on the bar at the Cross Keys with pickled onions and bread. He used to pour port in it.

Eddie Butcher

Raising Money

Uppingham used to be much smaller than it is now. It has grown a lot. During the war, Uppingham raised thousands and thousands of pounds for the Red Cross. The town was more like a big village when I was younger with a good community spirit. In those days we had Uppingham District Council and its own cattle market. The sheep and pigs were in the market place and the cattle were down by the station. That was up until the 1950s then they stopped the grading centre. During the war, the government bought all the livestock for meat and so you had to present it at a government grading centre and they graded and weighed it and sent a lot of it off by rail. There were three or four slaughterhouses in Uppingham at the time.

John Tabrum

The Ellingworth family lived in Melton Road, Oakham and had a music shop there. Harry was a photographer. From left to right, back row: George, Harry, Seth. Front row: Clara, Uncle Bill, Aunt Alice, Fanny.

The Fat Stock Show in Uppingham, c. 1900.

CHAPTER 9

People and Places

Tom Tabrum, John's father, outside his house in Uppingham just before the start of the Second World War.

Tom Tabrum

I can still see my grandfather, Tom Tabrum, now, sitting down to his breakfast. He'd have porridge with cream, then bacon, real fat, home-cured bacon which was fried, with eggs, fried bread, fried potatoes and anything else that would fry. Then he'd have toast and butter and marmalade. But he never spread the butter on the toast; he cut it in chunks and put it on the corner of the bread and put the marmalade on top. My mother used to say it was a good job we made our own butter. If we'd had to buy it he'd have eaten his ration in one sitting!

He worked every day and he took to his bed three weeks before he died at the age of eighty-four. He and Dick Clarke used to go off, every night, in Dick's car to look at somebody's cattle or go and see something else. Then they'd stop and have a whisky on the way home. They did that every night nearly in the summer and in the winter it would be two or three times a week.

He never seemed to be in a hurry, he'd always got time. He smoked a pipe and he enjoyed his drop of whisky. I remember he used to wear laced up boots and he used to have his pipe rack on a table by the fire where he used to sit. He'd sort out the pipe he was taking with him and then say, 'boy go fetch me boots'. Off I'd go and fetch his boots. Then they'd be off with their trilby hats and walking sticks.

John Tabrum

Horse Bus

My grandfather, Alfred Wadd Clarke, owned The Falcon in Uppingham at one time. He was always known as Dick Clarke. He used to run a horse bus to Manton Station and after that he ran the first motorised bus. He was a big, heavy man with a gammy leg because he was a bit arthritic. His greatest friend was old Tom Tabrum, John's grandfather. They used to go out together in the evenings, dressed like lords and both wearing their gold watch-chains. When I was sixteen or seventeen, I used to drive him about and I had to do the rounds. He had a few fields here and a few fields there and he'd always call in and see the local publicans. He

would go and do his shepherding and counting his sheep and this would be in the mornings and the evenings.

This was after he'd given up The Falcon. I remember going to the Marquis of Exeter at Lyddington which was nothing like it is now. It was just a tiny, little dark hole. We'd go to Lyddington, Bisbrook and round Castle Hill, Stretton and then back to Uppingham. His brother was Will Clarke and he kept the Crown Hotel. He had a very jolly daughter called Frances and on Thursdays, which was market day, she was always making Yorkshire pudding for the farmers who came in for their lunch. That was during the war and I don't think they cooked lunches at The Crown on other days.

Di Scott

Bramble

Mr and Mrs Hudson used to take in evacuees and when I first went to them there was still one lad left. His name was Terry Parsons and he used to muck about with us. I remember once we went blackberrying up the Spanoe aerodrome. In those days we all had short trousers but we could press the brambles down and climb over to get the berries without getting scratched. Terry was shorter than we were so he used to crawl underneath and end up in the middle. And then he couldn't get out! So we used to go across to people in the fields and ask them to help get him out. They used to come back with us, throw a coat over the brambles and lift him out. From then on he was called Bramble. Bramble was with us for

Thought to be Dick Clarke of Uppingham as a young man.

The singer, Matt Monroe, or Bramble as he was known in Luffenham. The photograph was taken in Great Yarmouth.

about six months and then he went back to London. When he was old enough he went on to be a bus driver and he eventually became Matt Monroe, the singer.

Alan Fox

The Rosebuds

Mrs Sharp lived in Dean Street and she ran The Rosebuds which was a dance club. We used to tap dance there. The practice room was in a room at a pub which I think was the Cross Keys.

Christine Baum

Yellow Cars

Lord Lonsdale was a character in the early 1930s. Cars in those days were nearly all black but Lord Lonsdale's cars were yellow, bright yellow. He had quite a fleet of them, Daimlers mainly. He even had one which was modified as a sort of closed-in pickup truck which carried a dozen hounds. He had a coach and four, painted yellow, with his coat of arms on the door. I remember on one occasion, perhaps in the 1920s, he drove up in his coach and four, for the meet with two footmen on the back.

Lord Lonsdale had a place near Oakham called Stone House. The story goes that he got a bit of lip from one of his footmen and he took him into his own boxing ring which he had in one of the rooms and took him on. This chap was rather good, probably better than Lord Lonsdale, but he patted him on the back afterwards and all was well. One of Lord Lonsdale's chauffeurs used to come into our pub and on one occasion my mother told him that I was going to London to stay with my grandmother in Chelsea. He offered to give me a lift so I went to London in a yellow Rolls Royce. We were going along the old Great North Road and there was a policeman standing at a crossroads with his bicycle. When he saw the yellow car coming he saluted.

Eddie Butcher

Pony Tricks

Jimmy Finch lived in Ayston Hall. He took my sister Clare and I to visit Lord Lonsdale at Stud House in Barleythorpe when we were quite small. He was very kind to us children and he had a pony that performed tricks and he got it to do some for us. Jimmy Finch had no children and he used to send for my sister and I when he had people for lunch and we'd knock on the door and he'd call, 'come in', and then introduce us as 'his children'. He used to play tricks on people and he loved to do naughty things. He had a gardener (or maybe he was a gamekeeper) and he put him on a horse and walloped it. The man couldn't ride and the horse jumped over the fence and into the stables. Jimmy Finch thought it was a huge joke but the poor man was terrified. He used to go shooting in Wardley Wood and once they put the pheasants in the tub and he set off at great speed. The back door of the tub flew open and the pheasants dropped out one by one. When he gave up riding he took to driving

this pony with a governess cart attached. It was a bit erratic.

Di Scott

The Pleasure Grounds

On the south terrace at Burley-on-the-Hill there were the Pleasure Grounds; they were the lawns and the herbaceous borders. From the Pleasure Grounds there were pathways down to Shibberty Freeze, and the Lion's Den which were play houses. There was a summer house and places for the children to play.

Ray Hill

Don Dismals

Mr Wilfred Finch was very kind but had the nickname Don Dismals. He had a fairly dark complexion with a narrow face and a moustache. The early Finches were the Earls of Winchelsea and the Earls of Nottingham who built the present house. The Mr Finch I knew died in 1939 and then the house was inherited by Colonel James Hanbury who was a nephew. He was tall with a Roman nose and was a proper gentleman.

During the wars the house was turned into a hospital. In the First World War it was used for officers suffering the effects of gas and in the Second World War it was a hospital for ordinary soldiers. They wore red, white and blue – blue suits, white shirts and red ties.

Ray Hill

Spotted Fly

Some of the characters who came into the Cross Keys in Oakham were a bit disreputable but they all had a nickname. There was one man we called the Spotted Fly. We don't know why. Another one was called Rabbits. He was probably a poacher because he always wore a raincoat with large pockets.

Eddie Butcher

Garden Boy

My dad was Lady Lonsdale's garden boy years ago down at Barleythorpe. He used to be at the front door by nine o'clock in the morning. He worked in the stables during the winter but in the summer when the horses were turned out, the stable lads worked in the garden. Eventually, Mr Finch at Burley-on-the-Hill wanted a gardener so instead of biking to Barleythorpe he went to work for Mr Finch.

Ray Hill

Roses

I was introduced by friends to my husband Alan, whose family owned the timber yard, R. and A.J. Rose, in North Luffenham. I met Alan in 1939 and he did not go into the army until 1942 because the timber business was a reserved occupation. We married in April 1945 just as the war was ending. I came to live here in a little house in the village when he eventually came home in 1946. The woodyard had been here since about 1860 and there have been Roses in the village since the 1600s although they were not timber merchants then.

Elsie Rose

Deliveries

Mr 'Scuttles' Burton had a pony and trap and he used to deliver parcels. He was a little man and he lived at the end of William Dolby Street.

Eileen Snow

Skating at Night

Burley-on-the-Hill was a grand country house near Oakham. It had a huge lake which froze over in the winter. At night cars drove round the lake and shone their headlights on to it and skating went on all night. That would be in the early 1930s. It was quite an occasion. They called the lake Burley Fishponds.

Eddie Butcher

Percy Stafford

My grandfather, Percy Stafford, was probably as much a character as anyone in the village. He was a jobbing builder and lived in Ketton all his life. You couldn't describe him as a rough diamond but he certainly wouldn't see anybody stuck. He could fix things. He was a fixer. He lived in Bull Lane and was part of a big family that lived on The Green in Ketton. His father was a stonemason for Hibbins.

Geoff Wright

Bertie, Bob and Alfie

The stone-waller for the Burley-on-the-Hill estate was Bertie Charity. He used to repair the Buckingham six-mile wall. Alfie Dawson was in the First World War and he lost the bottom part of his leg. When he came back he used to drive the estate lorry. He kept wicket for the cricket team so this wooden leg was quite useful. When they were bowling a bit fast he used to stick his leg out and stop the ball! Bob Appleyard, a keeper who lived down the Fishponds, was a really fast bowler. The Finches owned Burley Estate, Ravenstone, which is near Olney in Buckinghamshire and Eastwood in Kent. Burley used to play Ravenstone at cricket. It was always a needle match; we always had to win. Bob was a good cricketer, he used to put on his best show and bowl as fast as he could. One match, he bowled really fast and Alfie stuck his leg out to stop the ball, and his leg fell off! The visiting team couldn't understand it because they didn't know he had a wooden leg! Anyway, Alfie picked it up, and strapped it on again. In those days they used to have like a leather cup with wood at the bottom. There was a strap that Alfie strapped over his shoulder, and when his leg was back on, they carried on with the match.

Ray Hill

The Westmorelands

The Westmoreland family started a shop to sell wirelesses. He had five sons and Westmorelands became a chain store throughout the midlands. There was Ken Alwyn (who was in the town rugby team with me), Geoffrey, Ron and one other and they all ran a branch. The one daughter married Ben Hall and he eventually ran the branch in Oakham.

Eddie Butcher

Farmer Tarmar

Tarmar Lane got his name because when he was young he couldn't say 'farmer' so he said 'tarmar'. He used to tell us some tales.

Ray Hill

Glencoe Tubby

There was one farmer in Ketton who had a few milk cows, this was Glencoe Tubby. Glencoe was married and he and his sister ran the farm. We used to refer to his cows as Tubby's Shapes because they had bones sticking out all over. He used to walk them down the street morning and night. This was down the main road and sometimes they would compete with Skinner bringing his big herd in. The cattle used to make a mess along the road and it was always a source of great amusement to us kids if they did it outside the barber's shop! A car would go past and it would splash the glass and the barber, Ernie Fawkes, would come out and have an argument with Glencoe. Ernie Fawkes came from South Luffenham and he was a great character. The barber's shop was really a bit like the hub of the village. There couldn't have been many villages that had their own barbers. Gubber Walpole was the roadsweeper and he was always about Ketton. There was usually a feud going between him and Glencoe Tubby about the mess the cows made.

Geoff Wright

Nora

There were dances at the village hall but the Hudson's were very strict and I could only stay out until a certain time. There was a striking young girl who came over from Wakeley and we used to go over to the village hall at Barrowden where this young girl went. She was called Nora Regan and she was very good at table tennis. You guessed it, I married her!

Alan Fox

Lady Baden Powell

When I was a boy the Castle was used as the Assize Court. On one occasion, Lady Baden Powell came to talk to all the Guides and the Scouts and we all sat round in the castle grounds. I could never understand why there should be a horseshoe two feet across!

Eddie Butcher

Moving Around

In 1931 it was a very hard time. Ramsey Macdonald was Prime Minister and the country was almost bankrupt. We had to leave the pub but we had no debts. My mother had to go back to work as a cook. She was originally in service as a scullery maid at Marr Lodge which was built for Queen Victoria. She worked her way up and became a cook. She went to America with the people she worked for and she met my father, who was a butler, and they were married at The Little Church Round the Corner in New York. That was about 1912. In her time, she cooked for the old Princess Royal.

When they got rid of the pub they went together to Bisbrooke Hall. We had a little house in Oakham and they had someone to look after me so I continued at school and at weekends I would cycle over to Bisbrooke. Then my mother became a cook for the Orr-Ewings at Hambleton Manor and we had a little house there in the village so I could cycle into school from there every day.

Eddie Butcher

Remember to Curtsy

Mrs Cooper lived at the Manor House which was in between the Hall and the vicarage. She was a very formidable lady, I'm told, and was determined that Aggie Bushell should be postmistress at Hambleton – and she was! Mrs Cooper used to ride through the village in her carriage. The men were expected to doff their caps and the girls to curtsy. If they

Millie and Bert Hopper, John Tabrum, Tom and Olive Tabrum (John's parents), grandfather Tom Tabrum and May Toon.

didn't then they were unlikely to get their bag of coal at Christmas!

The part of the Manor House nearest to the vicarage had a flat roof. I'm told that Noel Coward used to stay there and at lunchtimes he used to perform for the children on that roof.

Dorothy Westland

128